Solving The Self-Esteem Puzzle

A Guide For Moving From Piece To Peace

Deborah Melaney Hazelton

Health Communications, Inc.
Deerfield Beach, Florida

Deborah M. Hazelton
InnerSight Unlimited
265 South Federal Highway, Suite 125
Deerfield Beach, FL 33441

© 1991 Deborah Melaney Hazelton
ISBN 1-55874-129-1

All rights reserved. Printed in the United States of America. No part of this
publication may be reproduced, stored in a retrieval system or transmitted in
any form or by any means, electronic, mechanical, photocopying, recording
or otherwise without the written permission of the publisher.

Publisher: Health Communications, Inc.
          3201 S.W. 15th Street
          Deerfield Beach, Florida 33442-8190

Cover design by Iris T. Slones

# DEDICATION

This book is dedicated to my guide dog Lyndi (trained with the SouthEastern Guide Dog School in Palmetto, Florida), who continues to be my nonsilent partner. Lyndi teaches me about the active and the passive aspects of what it means to love and be loved. She keeps me humble with her graciousness. She keeps me playful with her sense of humor and "eye" for a moment of joy. She keeps me responsible by exhibiting her own need for direction. Lyndi continues to be my teacher and my child, my "Spirit" incarnate.

ACKNOWLEDGMENTS

After I wrote the acknowledgment section for my last book, *The Courage To See: Daily Affirmations for Healing the Shame Within,* I realized it was my favorite section. Perhaps the reason why recovery and religion advocate gratitude so strongly is because it is so enlivening to the spirit within.

My life took on tremendous peace when I began to incorporate the "pieces" that have been given to me by the influence of special people and relationships over the years. It is impossible to list them all, but here are several who stand out in my mind as close friends, teachers, mentors, dreamers, role models and catalysts.

Special thanks to you each and all:

Jean Stanley, Joe and Mary Albrecht, Jill Boyd, Betty Potter, Lee Jones, Charles and Betty Lelly, Ann Gustin, Coleen Harmon, Beverly Whiteley, Marilyn Volker, Gayle Krause and Rick Alfaro.

Communicating via modem hooked up to my computers has greatly expanded my realm of possibilities, personal friendships and creative ideas over the past couple of years. Special thanks to Rick Alfaro and Kathy Fanning for influencing, teaching and supporting me through the learning process and formation of The InnerSight Connection bulletin board.

Special thanks to Ed Lawyer, a "free spirit," wonderful new friend and personal source of strength. By his creation and direction of *EchoNet,* a private telecommunications network, he has matched my dreams in this arena with a quality and genuine sense of community. My heart is full with renewed joy and peace!

Thanks also to Ed for supporting my formation and moderation of the *Safe Space Echo,* (a message base for personal support to individuals living with disabilities, or as I prefer to identify them, people who are "differently-abled"). To all of my *Safe Space* and *EchoNet* friends, my gratitude for letting me into your lives. Thanks also to Bonnie Lind for inviting me into *EchoNet* and for her love, support, fun and friendship.

And last but not least, to my friend and InnerSight Unlimited partner, Michael E. Miller, who encouraged this book from the beginning and guided me with extremely helpful direction. He has hung in there with me through the changes and still shows me, with humor and resourcefulness, that on a busy day, two half heads are better than one. Thank you, Michael, for your continued belief in me.

Debbie Hazelton

ᔆINTRODUCTION᠍ᔆ

As a young girl, I knew that finding, knowing and expressing myself were going to be the most important tasks in my life. If I wanted self-esteem, peace and harmony with others, I knew that I needed to work with the puzzle so that I could bring me out and let others in. And so it continues . . .

From Piece To Peace . . . That's how it goes as we move through the process of living and growing in making sense out of our lives. We experience, we learn, we become peace-filled until the next piece interrupts by crossing our paths, inviting us to understand still more.

Sometimes we are puzzled. Sometimes it seems as if we can never feel quite good enough. And so the quest for greater self-esteem continues. It is well that it should. After all, we are in our own company 24 hours a day. We talk a lot about growing in our capacity to love others. It only makes sense that we invest deeply in ourselves.

You hear and swallow messages. You ask questions. You carry doubts, make mistakes and succeed in accomplishments. You take risks, moving in the unknown . . . Whatever your experience, you are filled with the process and power of feeling fully alive and vital. Perhaps you express concern over the physical well-being of loved ones, and sometimes for the nutritional value of food. Why not give the same care to your self-esteem?

After all, you are your closest relationship.

Do you know that there is no such thing as too much self-love?

This means that you never have to worry about loving yourself too much. Certainly there are those who appear to love themselves too much, but this is only a high-energy exercise in false self-reassurance, if not self-deception.

When someone is really grounded in self-love, there is no need for self-convincing or putting on a show for others. So you have all the room you need to grow in self-esteem.

Solving the self-esteem puzzle is about moving through shame to a sense of integrity. It is about learning to make choices, setting boundaries. It is about finding balance in all aspects of your life.

How To Use This Book

What do you remember about books in your early days of school?

Do you remember when you got some of your first books — those that could actually be called your own? I remember feeling as if I belonged with other people in the world. I liked my books because they were *mine*.

Later as an adult in a tough time of change, I hunted for books that would speak to my experience. When I located some at last, I felt validated and less isolated.

This is a guide for you, for sorting and solving the self-esteem puzzle. It is a housing, a safe place for you to sift and sort through your experiences, values and choices. Work with it in a way that makes sense to you. Use it privately or choose with whom you want to share it. Either way, keep in mind that it is for your expression.

If the thought of sharing it with someone else means that you would watch and weigh your words, then save it just for you. You may write in it, draw in it, bend it, hide it in a special place, take it with you wherever you choose . . . It is yours! Use it in a place where no one can literally look over your shoulder. In time, that sense of someone looking over your shoulder from inside you will minimize. This book is not meant to take the place of therapy, but may be a supportive place to clarify what is in your life as you go through the process of therapy.

If you're a curious person, you may want to read right through this book once, then come back to the beginning and take your time with each section. This is a place to savor your experience. It is a safe place for exploring your life, brainstorming options for possible changes.

In the first section, "I Am" is the focus. This is a time to broaden self-awareness, to pay attention to your experience of and with yourself. This is a place to notice those voices in your head, those taped messages you continue to hear. It is a time to build self-nurturance and balance.

Part Two focuses on relationships and ways that we continue to simultaneously serve as teachers and students for one another. Relationships can contribute to positive feelings of self-worth, thereby enhancing self-esteem, yet can also contribute to lowering self-esteem and erode your sense of self-worth. You continue to make choices in your relationships with people, conscious or unconscious, that affect your self-esteem.

In Part Three, Places And Things, the focus is on your relationships with your environment. How do you feel about everything from the place where you live, money, your job to the music you hear? How do you interact with your environment that adds to or subtracts from your self-esteem?

And finally, Part Four, The School Of Life, is where you put it all together. What underlying beliefs do you carry about why you're here in this life? What work do you have yet to finish in life's lessons? How can you look at your life today so that you know throughout the complexity of your experience, that you make sense?

You make sense. That is one of the most important components to gaining and maintaining genuine self-esteem. Those seemingly wayward pieces of your life fit into a puzzle that, when solved, is your guide to peace because you are whole. This does not mean that you and I are always right, or always pleased with the results of our lives. But it does mean that there is continuity between our experience and the outcome of that experience as it manifests in our lives. It means that all of the pieces of that puzzle called "you" do fit together into your whole complete person.

I wish for you the gentle appreciation and vision to know that you and your life do make sense, and that the pieces of your own puzzle continue leading you to peace in your life.

May you feel loved to peace.

Deborah M. Hazelton

Contents

PART I

"I Am"

Image

The way you see yourself — or self-image — is reflected back to you constantly. Your reaction to this reflection can tell you a lot about your self-esteem.

If you expect to truly love others, you need to start by first learning to love yourself. This is not a shameful venture, but a joyous opportunity. It can feel very scary, especially in those parts of our lives where we have carried a lot of shame. "What? I goofed again? I didn't love myself enough!" Damned if you do and damned if you don't.

Janet Woititz tells us in *Adult Children Of Alcoholics* that adult children "guess at what's normal." So it is when we are trying to figure out exactly how to relate with ourselves. So if you have values about treating others in loving, respectful ways, why would you treat yourself any differently?

---

*Janet Woititz *Adult Children of Alcoholics* (Deerfield Beach, FL: Health Communications, 1983; rev. 1990.)

1

My Self-Esteem Bank Account

How much do you have in your self-esteem bank account? Probably more than you realize. You have accumulated a pool of resources that is there for your use. You can find strength and wisdom from many places in your life. Your resources, your richness in spirit nourish your self-esteem and self-care. When it comes to reaching a thorough understanding of the past, you don't have to throw out the baby with the bath water. Though you have had pain and disappointment, there is much you have survived and accomplished.

The hard times — the times when you've needed defenses, pride, sarcasm, anger, stubbornness — can also turn out to be assets. Those things have worked for you, have helped you survive. Yes, they have probably also worked against you; but finding that balance and making those choices is all part of growing in self-esteem.

So why not periodically take stock of your accumulated resources, just as you would look at your bank account? What's your overall account balance? Do you have an available balance that shifts from day to day? This available balance is your current self-esteem.

Why isn't more of your overall account balance available to you? Who is withholding some of your resources? Could it be you? Why? What can you do to make even more of your own resources available to you?

The Mystery Of The Dipper And The Bucket

I found the following story in a pile of material given to me by a colleague. Use this metaphor to approach your self-esteem and take stock of your own available resources:

You have heard the story of the cup that overflows. This is the story of a bucket that is like that cup, only larger, and it is invisible. We each have a bucket, and it is always with us. The amount of self-esteem in our bucket determines how we feel about ourselves and about others, and how we get along with people.

Have you ever experienced a series of very favorable events that make you want to be good to people for a week? When this happens, your bucket is full to overflowing.

Your bucket can be filled by a lot of things. When people speak to you, recognizing you as a human being, your bucket is filled a little; it is filled even more if they call you by name. If they compliment you on your dress or a job well done, the level in your bucket will go up still higher. There must be a million ways to raise that level in another person's bucket.

But remember, this is a theory about a *dipper* and a bucket. Other people have dippers, and they can get their dippers into your bucket.

Let's say I'm at a banquet — nice tablecloth, china, silverware. Everyone is dressed up. I inadvertently upset my cup of coffee. A big brown spot appears on the tablecloth, steam rises, the stain begins to crawl across the table. Finally, it dribbles over the other side onto a woman's lap, and she jumps because the coffee is hot.

I'm now so embarrassed that I'd like to stop the world and get off. And then the man sitting right next to me says, "Do you know you upset your coffee?"

I made a mistake, and I knew it first. Then he said, "You upset your coffee." He got his dipper in my bucket.

Buckets are filled and buckets are emptied. And when our bucket is empty, we are very different from when our bucket is full.

If you say to a woman whose bucket is empty, "That's a very pretty dress you're wearing today," she will reply, "What the heck was wrong with the dress I wore yesterday?"

The interplay of the dipper and the bucket is the story of our lives, and everyone has both. The mystery of the dipper and the bucket is this. The only way we can fill our own bucket is to fill someone else's bucket.

The next time someone is right about what is wrong with you when you know it, you can say, "Hey, you've got your dipper in my bucket!"

Or, better yet, when you hear others saying what they think is wrong with somebody else, you can say, "We're getting our dippers in this person's bucket, and we ought to be filling instead of dipping." In doing this you can experience the mystery of the dipper and the bucket.

Reflections On The Mystery

We can't fill our own buckets or get other people to fill them as long as we are dipping. And usually, when we are dipping from the buckets of others, we are also allowing others to dip from our own.

So how about you? Can you look at your life and see your self-esteem in a bucket? What is the size of your bucket? What is it made of? How old is your current bucket? What is the level in your bucket right now? What was it like yesterday? Can you think of anything that happened today to raise or lower that level?

As long as we're on this planet, we will respond to things said to us, to things said about us, and to what we say to ourselves about our own self-worth. While we may wish to have that level stay constant, it always fluctuates. Growing in self-esteem is about getting beyond the shame, about low self-esteem. It is a big step to admit that your self-esteem is sometimes low or struggling.

On some days I am tempted to wonder if someone has put a hole in the bottom of my bucket! On other days I find it hard to know what is really in my bucket. How about you?

Then there are those dippers: putdowns, critical remarks, insults, assuming remarks that discount or diminish you. Some of my dippers are people who ignore what I'm saying. What are some of the dippers you most often experience? Can you attach names of people to these dippers?

_____

_____

Finding those people and giving names to those dippers isn't about blame. Blaming feeds shaming, and two wrongs don't make a right. As we are dipped, we are tempted to dip in return in order to try and get back what someone else has taken. Instead, we can be aware. We can work with our own consciousness so that those people don't have so much access to our buckets with their dippers. We can grow in our role of being more fully in charge of our own bucket, and clearer about what those dippers are as we experience their effects.

A friend once told me that she would frequently say to her children after they were hurt by what someone said: "Are you going to let that person walk around in your head with their dirty feet?" So now I ask you: Are you going to let those people bring their dippers and continue to take out of your bucket of self-esteem?

The secrecy of shame diminishes as we realize that we are not alone with this challenge. Fortunately, as we grow in awareness, we can also grow in the size of the bucket we carry. Those things in your life that you used to view as ugly warts, that fed into your feeling of shame, may turn out to be precious gems added to your bucket. In turn, what you used to define as dippers may also change, and may continue to do so over the years.

Can you think of any dippers that used to get under your skin that you now find humorous? How about dippers that just don't phase you anymore? Some dippers may become less important as we learn not to give our power away to others, and some may become less important as we grow in trust.

Remember that the goal here is not to add up the dippers, but to have more self-esteem in your bucket. The dippers are signals that the level in your bucket may be getting low, or that it's time to find more ways to maintain and grow in self-esteem.

Finding Buried Treasures For Your Bank Or Bucket

What have you learned from life experience?

From living in chaos, I learned _____

_____

From living with conflict, I learned _____

_____

From being violated, I have learned _____

_____

From watching or experiencing the effects of alcohol or drugs, I have

learned _____

_____

From irresponsibly displaying anger, I have learned _____

_____

From not dealing with anger, I have learned _____

_____

From having defenses, I have learned _____

_____

From keeping secrets, I have learned _____

_____

From trusting people with secrets, I have learned _____

_____

From my stubbornness, I have learned _____

_____

From pride, I have learned _____

_____

From grief, I have learned _____

_____

From loving another person, I have learned _____

_____

From being overly critical of myself, I have learned _____

_____

From the sources of shame in my life, I have learned _____

_____

From relationships that did not work, I have learned _____

_____

From people I felt betrayed, abandoned or let down by, I have learned

_____

From my own experience at rejecting others, I have learned _____

_____

From my decisions to say no to the desires or demands of others, I have

learned _____

_____

_____

Here are some of my reflections that may add to your own thoughts. Take
what you like and leave the rest:

From crisis, I learned to be flexible.
From abuse, I learned to pay attention to signals.
From defenses, I learned to protect myself.
From self-protection, I learned I have self-esteem that is worthy of my
attention.

And from all of life, I grow in wisdom and in strength.
What are some other things you learned from life experiences?

_____

_____

_____

Things I Like About Myself Today

Now you've looked at some of the strengths you've brought with you.
Perhaps many of them have come out of difficult times. Like the fine possessions we have, which cannot all possibly get used on a daily basis, many of
the resources you are discovering that are yours to draw upon may not
immediately come to mind or to your day-to-day use. Nevertheless, they are
still treasures that go with you in your bucket.

One of the best ways to get a sense of what's in your bucket right now is to think of what you like about yourself today.

You spend a lot of time with this person we call by your name. You have a relationship with this person. What do you like about (fill in the blank with your name). What do you like about who this person is?

"I like _____'s sensitivity."

"I like _____'s humor."

"I like _____'s honesty."

"I like _____'s determination and willingness to grow and change."

"I like _____'s stubbornness."

"I like the way _____ holds fast to and honors his/her perceptions and experience."

"I like the way _____ spoils himself/herself by being lazy."

"I like how hard _____ has worked to survive, find meaning, and be who he/she is."

"I like _____'s vulnerability."

"I like the trail, the path, that always shows that the pieces in _____

_____'s life do make sense."

"I like the way _____ holds back when something doesn't feel right."

"I like _____'s loyalty."

"I like _____'s kindness toward others."

"I like _____'s moodiness; it shows she/he is real."

Other things I like:

_____

_____

_____

How does it feel to notice those things? It's as if you're noticing things about a friend, isn't it?

Now go back to these things you've dared to notice. Take out your name and replace it with "my."

Now read the sentences again. Try saying them out loud.

How does that feel? Are you nervous? Do you feel silly? Do you feel silly when you notice what you like about a friend? Are you surprised to find more than you expected about those things you are liking about yourself?

Things I Like About What I've Done Today

Those are traits. Let's get even more concrete and look specifically at behaviors.

What do you like about what you've done today? What do you like about what you've done over the last week? Can you think of some things you feel especially good about?

Sometimes it is easier to think in small steps, about concrete things you are noticing today, yesterday, last week. We spend so much time in personal growth and recovery talking about early childhood. Sometimes it's refreshing to simply start with today.

Each time you can recognize ways in which you like yourself, that self-esteem goes into your bucket or bank account. And while it may seem commonplace to praise friends, we deserve self-praise in our lives in order to nurture self-esteem.

Being And Doing

We've looked at characteristics you like, and we've looked at behaviors you like. But we don't want to get stuck in doing versus being. If you praise yourself only for what you do, then you may only feel you're okay or good enough so long as you're accomplishing things. If you praise yourself for who you are and not for what you do, you could be spinning your wheels for a long time, staying stuck in "not doing."

We need to find a balance between what we do and who we are, and we need praise from ourselves. Remember, we are with ourselves day in and day out. Who deserves our attention and needs our praise more?

Louise Hay suggests saying to yourself, "I approve of myself." Perhaps this is a beginning to self-praise. Let's look at praise for being and for doing.

Being: "I really like who I am." "It's really wonderful that I've grown so much in my intuitiveness . . . my self-trust . . . my self-esteem. I have grown in substance, in character, and often, just by doing nothing, just learning to be me."

Doing: "I like the job I did today on _____." "I am so proud of myself for the things I have accomplished. They include _____."

There is a T-shirt that says, "I may not be perfect, but parts of me are excellent." Remember: Self-praise is noticing the aspects of yourself that are excellent, even in the face of imperfection. There will always be imperfection, particularly as long as there continues to be human risk. But parts of you are excellent, particularly in your spirit, your vulnerability. You deserve your self-praise.

Try it, and notice how much easier it becomes to carry a bucket that is filling rather than emptying. Notice how those dippers can't get to you as easily. And notice, too, that you're not as tempted or as likely to scrounge around in someone else's bucket with your dippers as you grow in your own self-praise.

"Facing" The Mirror

Many self-help books talk about the importance of "looking in the mirror." Why do you suppose they do that?

In part, it has to do with our visual society. How do you decide who you want to be around? Does it sometimes have to do with looks or physical presence or attractiveness? When something seems wrong about someone, do you often comment first on how something doesn't "look quite right"? Even without and beyond visual perceptions, we all have feelings about our physical bodies. We make judgments about the physical attractiveness of others, and we often take for granted our own physical appearance and ignore our own self-perceptions. Having a relationship with ourselves that fosters and maintains healthy self-esteem begins with loving our bodies, greeting ourselves, acknowledging our own presence to ourselves. The mirror is a good place to start.

How do you feel when you look in the mirror? What do you say to yourself?

I say, "_____"

I feel _____.

"I wonder what to do about _____"

"I wonder if I would be more loved if I could get rid of _____

_____"

I feel silly because _____.

I feel stupid when _____.

Here are some alternate answers:

"Oh yuck!"	"Hi There!"
"I look so ugly!"	"Oh I look great!"
"Damn! I hate my face!"	"I love you!"

Are you laughing nervously as you read the left-hand column? Do you feel squeamish when you read the column on the right?

When you see the faces of loved ones, do you say, "Oh yuck! You are so ugly?" All too often we assume that self-love is not okay. But if self-love is not okay, then how can we expect to have the resources to love others? We are with ourselves more than we are with anyone else. It is our own love and support we need first and foremost.

Practice looking in the mirror. Continue to breathe as you see yourself. Consider all of the situations in your life that you have already "faced." Give yourself credit as you "face" yourself, for carrying a body that continues to carry you.

My Sexuality

My sexuality is very private and subjective. The most important part of it is what I experience between my ears.

It is not surprising that closet doors that have long hidden the shame and pain of sexual abuse are opening. As we work to build self-esteem, it becomes increasingly important to clear away pain that impedes positive feelings toward ourselves and our lives.

Sexual abuse is probably the deepest violation. It is an invasion of the most personal parts of our bodies, and it defies our every effort to have a will of our own in choosing who will touch us and how we will be touched. Exploring sexuality creates the opportunity to challenge every fear of intimacy. The violation of sexual abuse invites us to challenge every personal reflection of shame we have carried.

Your Experience

What has your experience been with respect to feeling sexually safe? Was violation a part of your early experience? Have you carried a history, a "herstory," of feeling sexually violated?

Discovering who you have felt violated by or how you have felt violated may help you become grounded in your experience. If the memories come, let them and the feelings that go with them be part of your experience. Claiming your feelings and any memories that come to mind is all part of what will help you claim or reclaim your own sense of personal power.

If you find a lot of surfacing anger, use it as energy to help you make the changes you wish in moving forward. Your anger and grief can signal you to affirm your self-worth. Actually, anger is an indication that you already have more self-worth than you may have realized. Fear can help you move into expressing vulnerability. Any and all of these pieces can help you make conscious the messages that have influenced you and continued to eat at your self-esteem.

From this point of awareness, you can become grounded in choosing new messages. You do not need to know who abused you, or how, in order to determine that your experience is valid. For some, re-experiencing early memories of abuse is a positive step in overcoming the shame and old pain. For others, this step of remembering and re-experiencing is not essential. Memories can help. They can also be a place for getting stuck. Some people find it easier and safer to stay in the memories, rather than move through them and on with living.

Messages

It's not as important as you may think to be able to recall details. A major key to memory is housed in the "messages" that you have been given, which you carry and live out.

"Okay," you may be tempted to say, "I got in touch with some of the messages I've been carrying. I know they're there. I know they affect me. I don't want them."

And so you are tempted to drop them like a hot potato! It's also tempting to blame others for giving you those messages.

A wonderful game described through the transactional analysis model is called, "See what you made me do?" We have the illusion that somehow, if we can hold someone else responsible, we can let go of what we don't want to be ours.

But if you've carried it, no matter from what source it came, it is yours — at least until you really get rid of it. You might think that finding someone to blame is a way to pass it on and get rid of it, to save face, to disown responsibility for any part of the shame or the sham. But keep in mind that "Blaming feeds shaming." If you need to give someone your power in order for you to have permission to claim your experience, then you will always need those memories and that old pain to determine your self-worth.

What are the messages you got as a child about what to expect sexually?

"Sex is dirty, save it for the one you love."

"When you marry and have children . . ."

"Your body is not your own. You must learn to cooperate with others by giving up your will."

" 'Relax' is a signal that pain is about to begin."

"You're not a sexual person and therefore are no good to anyone."

"You are here to be sexual in order to please people and be worthwhile."

"Don't masturbate or you'll go blind."

"Don't be one of those people."

"Do it the right way or there must be something wrong with you."

What did you learn about your body?

As a child, you were told _____

_____ about your body.

What was your body like?

How was it referred to?

To whom did it belong?

If you are a woman, what words did you hear for your vulva?

pussy

potty

cunt

snatch

pocketbook

nookie

crotch

vulvo

down there

your privates

List others here: _____

If you are a man, what words did you hear for your penis?

prick

dick

cock

tally wag

wang

ding-dong

thing-a-ma-bob

George, Ralph, Mr. Happy or some other name

thing

tally-wacker

pee-pee

wee-wee

your privates

List others here: _____

What were you told about genitals?

their purpose

their use

your joy about them

your behavior with them

your fear of them

What words did you hear for breasts?
    bosoms
    watermelons
    raisins
    boobs
    boobies
    tits
    hooters
    gazumbas
    List others here: _____

What words did you hear for buttocks?
    fanny
    bummie
    rear end
    ass
    posterior
    rump
    butt
    backside
    derriere
    bum
    List others here: _____

What word did you hear for urination?
    weewee
    piss
    pee
    golden showers
    taking a leak
    bleeding the dragon
    gotta see a man about a horse
    doin' your business
    List others here: _____

What word did you use for defecation?
    crap
    shit
    big job
    making dumplings
    having a B.M.
    having a bowel movement
    taking a dump
    feces

  doin' your business
  number 2
  List others here: _____

Some of the same words that are used for getting angry, such as "getting pissed off," are used for bodily functions. And how often do we hear or say something about "getting our shit together"? If we're really working with self-esteem, then why would we want to get something together that is also the word for feces? After all it is our body's waste. Our words act as mirrors that reflect our own self-perceptions.

We deserve to respect and love our bodies through our language. Learning to know and use the right words in our adulthood is an active way to respect the goodness of our bodies and the richness of their continuous functioning. (On the other hand, perhaps balance is a key here. I once heard of a boy who was given so many right words for body parts that he began to refer to his "pagina"!)

What were you told about same-sex feelings?

  It's bad.
  It's sick.
  It's dirty.
  Don't ever let me catch you . . .
  It's delayed adolescence.
  It's role confusion.
  It's a phase.
  You'll grow out of it.

What is your own private experience with same-sex feelings?

_____

_____

_____

What were you told about opposite-sex feelings?

  Don't scare anyone away.
  Wait until you finish school.
  When you marry . . .
  When you have children . . .

What is your own private experience about opposite-sex feelings?

_____

_____

_____

What were you told about personal boundaries?

  Nothing, I wasn't encouraged to have them.

I wasn't supposed to touch myself.

I got mixed messages.

I was told to create, maintain and respect boundaries, both my own and those of others.

What was your experience? Was it different than what you were verbally told? Did you hear one thing and experience another?

_____

_____

_____

What other messages can you think of that are particularly yours? You can add more here at any time.

_____

_____

_____

There is a dance between feeling violated and isolated. It has to do with feeling that one or more people didn't honor your personal boundaries and simultaneously were not emotionally available to you. So your life, your boundaries, your right to privacy were open to them — you could not safely turn outward for comfort. The "dance" goes something like:

"I was violated.

"I was abandoned by anyone who noticed and discounted my feelings and experience.

"It is safe to remain isolated.

"And I am hungry for love, validation, healing and mirrors that tell me I'm okay.

"So it hurts to come out of hiding, and it hurts to stay alone. Oh, if only they would love me so I could heal! But if they stop touching me, I might not feel loved at all!"

It's a bind, a very real one. It became a decision to stay alone rather than to risk violation or abandonment. Being alone means life remains predictable, safe. Being alone means not having to risk being exposed, humiliated or betrayed. It also means remaining apart from companionship, the healing that comes from being loved. It means that new information is never available for old and new challenges. Instead, old answers and decisions are recycled over and over to meet life's difficulties. It's kind of like playing a card game over and over and wondering why you keep coming up with the same hand. Somehow, when the cards are dealt, you end up feeling as if you can only play the same cards. Perhaps you even try to play more advanced games, yet only believe you can play those games, those hands, with the same limited number of cards. Somewhere along the line it became too scary, inconceivable perhaps, to learn other strategies.

Can you plug this metaphor into your life in some way? Are there situations where you're still using the same old answers? Treating new people like the old people of your past? Responding today with yesterday's anger? Assuming the same lack, the same abandonment that happened yesterday will again happen tomorrow?

Have you ever heard the story about the woman who always cut the ends off a ham before she put it into the baking pan? When someone asked her why she did it that way, she replied, "That's the way my mother did it." When her mother was asked why she did it, she responded, "Because that's the way *my* mother did it." Finally, the trail of questions got back to a great-grandmother who said, "Why, I *had* to cut the ends off — that was the only way the ham would fit into the pan!"

The original answer to the challenge was accurate for that moment in time. But perhaps some of the ways you are answering your life now are answers that deserve to be put away, remembered as treasured solutions for the day in which they were vital and useful answers.

Perhaps playing with new cards is scary because it's hard to know where to begin. Trying on new behaviors and testing out different strategies mean taking risks, but remember: It doesn't have to, can't, won't be done overnight. Be gentle with yourself!

Little Steps

"I take little steps. I let myself out in small ways that create space within and around me for others to come into my life. I create space so that the strength and love of others can help me feel safe to come out of hiding."

Perhaps these and other phrases will help you feel gentle toward yourself while daring, ever so slightly to take little steps.

Some Ways I Can Take Risks

- I initiate a conversation with someone new today.
- I take time to talk to someone I usually ignore.
- I take time to listen to what someone else is saying. I pay attention to the feelings of someone else today and listen beyond their words.
- I risk disagreeing with someone today and find it is safe, that there is room for more than one viewpoint.
- I tell someone something about what I like today.

- I reach out and physically touch someone today.
- I find something to say no to today.

What other risks can you think of to add? Dare to mention what has not yet been mentioned. If it exists in your mind and heart, it is valid.

Your Body

Your body carries you around day after day, year after year. Yet we often carry secrets, pockets of negative feelings, about our bodies.

Draw a picture of your body. Use a pencil, crayon or anything else you can make a mark with and have some fun! If you don't want to draw, then find some scissors, paste and whatever objects you can use to build with. This is not an art contest. What will be important through this process is how you feel about yourself.

Remember looking in the mirror? Now notice how you feel as you draw or recreate your body. Do you find this to be a fun activity? How do you feel about your size? What are you doing to show your size? Do you allow yourself to take up space in the universe? Do you draw yourself as all middle? As spindly? Keep in mind that this is about how you feel, not some textbook interpretation.

Notice those areas of the body where you feel comfortable. Also notice — simply notice — those areas, if any, where you may experience any discomfort in how you depict various parts of yourself.

Likes And Dislikes

Typically, we notice what we like and dislike about others: their looks, their voices, their ways. Yet we often remain secretive or silently ashamed about our own bodies and what we like and dislike.

Imagine you have an opportunity to trade in old body parts for new ones.

What would you keep?

Why?

What would you trade in?

Why?

What would you wish to have instead?

Why?

What would it do for you?

List three adjectives about the parts of your body you would trade in.

_____

_____

_____

List three adjectives about the parts of your body you would keep.

_____

_____

_____

Getting Acquainted

When you approach a new friend, how do you reach out? Do you take time to establish rapport? Do you respect that it takes time to build trust, to become comfortably familiar?

So it is with your body and how you and others relate to and with your body.

Take yourself on a tour of your body. Start by holding your hand. Is your right hand holding your left? Vice versa? Now switch. Notice both experiences: as your hand is felt or held, and as your other hand holds and caresses. Massage your hands together. Do you have a favorite body lotion you can use to add to this experience? Travel up your arms if you like, and notice how you feel about touching yourself.

Now rub your feet. Are they usually ticklish when someone touches them? How about when you touch them? Do you like to be stroked between your toes? How about around the back of your foot, the ball of your foot, your instep and your heel? How do you feel now about touching your feet? Are they dirty? Do you want to wash all this off your hands? Remember that your feet carry you around, day after day.

Now let your hands travel up your legs in gentle, massaging motions. Does this feel good to you?

Now come back up and massage your shoulders. Rub your neck and think about all the people and situations that you've referred to as a "pain in the neck" lately. Is there pain in your neck now? Can you find ways to rub your neck that now feel good to you?

Do you like to have your head rubbed? Remember that the brain in your head does a lot of thinking, problem-solving and idea-popping for you, day after day.

Do you like to have your face rubbed, stroked? Experiment and see if you can find out some specifics about what you do and don't like.

Now explore your body further. How do you feel as you touch your stomach? It holds the food that nourishes your body. Many people complain about their stomachs. Do you like yours? Does it feel good to have your stomach rubbed?

How about your chest? Do you carry a lot of tension there? Is there something you need to "get off your chest"? How about your breasts? Men and women both have breasts, and men and women each vary as to what they like done with their breasts. So listen to your own individual response as you explore and find out what you like.

How do you feel about your genitals? If it is right for someone else to love them, and it makes sense to grow in self-esteem, then how can it be "not okay" to touch them yourself? Do you know how you like them touched? Are they familiar to you? Do you know how they work? Do you care?

Don't forget to touch your face, your hands, your toes, your teeth. How do you feel about saliva? It keeps your mouth from getting too dry, so you can grow in confident self-expression. Saliva helps to wash down the food that nourishes your body, keeping you fit to participate in the world.

How do you feel about bodily waste?

It is nature's divine way of helping to get rid of what you no longer need to carry around. Do you know that everyone does indeed pass gas? Call it what you like, attempt to ignore it, but we all do it. Is that yet another taboo?

How do you feel about fingernails? Toenails? Nails can help to open things. They can be a place to display pride in our appearance.

As you touch your body, notice the following:

What feels good?
What don't you like?
What sounds do you notice?
What images do you notice?

Body Care

I take care of my body. I actively choose food that is nourishing for me. I move my body in ways that use and respect my muscles. I listen to bodily signals of what feels good and what doesn't:

with food
with touch
with clothes
with movement

List foods you would be better off eating less of:

What do you get out of continuing to eat these foods that are not good for you? Is there a payoff? Do you get something emotionally? Do you stuff down anger? Comfort old grief? Feel a sense of companionship? Do you get to feel awful later and less able to manage your life? What other things?

List healthy foods you would like to eat more of:

_____

_____

What would this do for you? What benefits would eating healthier food have on your daily life? What would this do for your spirit? Your mental capability? Your emotions? Your energy level? What other benefits can you imagine?

_____

_____

List some things you would like to do for your body:
Get regular massages.
Do regular exercise.
Go for regular walks, swimming, bike riding.
Explore holistic health care and/or eating habits.

Self-Talk

It used to be said that people who talk to themselves are crazy, and even crazier if they answer themselves! But like breathing, everyone has to do it at one time or another — it's part of how we maintain our sanity. The craziness is if there is *no* self-talk.

Self-talk, aloud or silent, can be a private conversation. The more we answer and talk back to ourselves, the better. Talking to and answering ourselves puts us more at the center of our relationship to ourselves.

But to do this we need to be in the driver's seat of our self-talk. Unfortunately, we tend to replay messages in our heads as though we're watching old movies, playing old tapes. We insert new people, new props into old memories, hearing old scripts we've heard many times over. We hear these messages, and relive the same old familiar feelings in our bodies, playing out our reactions to these messages in our relationship to ourselves and to the details of our daily lives.

You have a right to take active responsibility for the messages that play in your head. Some people move away from violent TV, violent life situations. Some move away from toxic food and other environmental influences. You have a right to move away from statements in your head that are not good for you, and to turn up the volume on messages that feed and nourish your self-esteem.

Remember, we're talking here about the self-talk statements that you make privately to yourself in your own head. Some people refer to these voices as "the committee" or "the group" because they know there are parts of themselves in debate, or because they know that several old voices of the past are still interfering with their present ability to feel attuned to and at peace with themselves today.

So give conscious thought and gentle respect to the voices and messages you allow to play in your head. When you make a mistake and are tempted to put yourself down by calling yourself "stupid" or various other potent adjectives and nouns, think of how you would treat people you care about when they make a mistake. You deserve the same kindness.

Affirmations

Affirmations are popular tools for working with our thoughts. To affirm something is to make it solidly true. Affirmations are like training wheels. They help us to feel more secure in the mind-set we desire, while we build muscle memory and skill to achieve the desired results naturally. Affirmations are not meant to be used as a brainwashing mechanism. They are not meant to encourage changing feelings through a pep talk. They are a tool, but one that has much artistic possibility for helping to shape our mental landscape.

Tone is important. Have you ever heard someone use what sounded like "the right words" but something was still missing? Your intuitive child within knows when something doesn't feel true. The words "I love you," "I'm here for you," or "Call if you need something" are caring words. But if you say them in an unfriendly, impersonal tone, which part — the words or the tone — do you hear more loudly in your head? You hear the tone every time. So it is in using affirmations. The tone you use can make or break your outcome.

As the old saying goes, "You can catch more flies with honey than you can with vinegar." Say affirmations gently and calmly. Using them intensely or harshly is a mere reflection of shame in disguise. Think of it this way: Do the old messages of when you were judged or punished still replay in your head? Do you hear not only the words, but also the tone? As a child this tone gave you the feeling that you were not okay. Your subconscious feels and responds to that tone when you urgently pound away at affirmations. That child part of yourself won't be fooled by your attempts at pounding something into your belief system. It only adds to a kind of inner warfare, and that is energy draining. If you are tempted to impatiently beat yourself up with affirmations, you might check out whether you are still coming from a shame base, reflecting the tone by which you heard messages about who and how you were supposed to be.

Remember to breathe when you say affirmations: slow, rhythmic and full breathing. No room for hyperventilation here! It's important to relax so that the good can become believable throughout your body. Your body carries you around day after day. It needs to feel supported by your words and thoughts so that it can continue to house your dreams, your activities, your mobility as you live your life.

Relax

I used to become guarded when anyone told me to relax. I took it as a sign that someone was about to do something to me that I would not like.

What memories do you have of the word or notion of what it means to "relax"?

But that was then, and this is now. "Relax" is a word you can say almost rhythmically. Hear yourself say in your head "re" when you inhale, and "lax" when you exhale. If you tend to hyperventilate, the word alone cannot invite you to become calm and peaceful. Have you ever heard anyone yell, "Relax!"? What did it do? Cause you to be more tense? Of course.

When you say your affirmations, you are creating an atmosphere, a seedbed for the garden of your self-esteem to blossom into fruition. The roots are important, and so is the atmosphere. Balance. There is no point in drowning or overwhelming yourself with pep-talk pushiness!

Affirmations are positive. They are centered in the present. Take that wish-list and project some realistic portion of it into the present: "I wish I had money" translates into: "I have the money I need." Or, "I am open to ideas and opportunities for attracting the money I need and desire in new ways."

Affirmation Viewpoint

Here's an exercise taken from a self-esteem workshop with Jack Canfield: Write an affirmation for yourself and notice how you feel. Example: "I am a loving and worthwhile person with a lot to offer other people."

What do you feel when you write that?

"Ha! What a joke!"

"People wouldn't say that if they knew me."

"Yes, that is true!"

"I'm learning to accept that this is so."

What happens if someone tells you: "You are a loving and worthwhile person with a lot to offer other people."

Did you hear that? Imagine different people you know saying that. You are a loving and worthwhile person. You! How do you feel when you hear that? What statements come to mind?

"What do you want?"

"You wouldn't say that if you really knew me."

"Thank you for noticing."

"I like hearing that."

Write it again, and notice what comes up. This is a way to flush out those projections and perceptions we secretly carry and assume in the corners of our minds.

Now imagine that someone is saying this about you to someone else:

"(Your name) _____ is such a loving and worthwhile person. He/she has so much to offer other people."

"Have you noticed how much (your name) _____ has to offer others? Have you noticed how loving and worthwhile he/she is?"

You're being talked about by someone. What does that other person say in response?

"I know it! And I hope (your name) knows how much he/she gives."

"I hope (your name) knows how worthwhile he/she is."

"Ha! You've got to be kidding! Her? Him?"

Perhaps these statements call to mind specific people in your life, and how you remember being talked about, or how you imagine being spoken of. What's important here are the perceptions you carry. Who comes to mind is important and can be noted for later work on relationships. But here it is important to know that you carry these perceptions and you can change them.

Write your affirmation again from any point of view and look at the underlying messages. Remember to be gentle with yourself. You can quietly shift away from all those "others" in your head and gently work with positive statements at any time. Remember, the goal we're after here is positive self-talk, which is an important component of self-esteem.

Suggested Affirmations

"I'm okay as I am."

"I'm more than my mistakes."

"There's more to who I am than the old tapes in my head would indicate."

"I deserve good things in my life."

"I am loved."

"I deserve a life of abundance."

"Now I am reaping without ruining."

"I am slightly willing to change, trusting that the universe will do the rest to bring about its continual perfect order."

Now go back to the mirror and think about your reaction to what you've been learning about self-talk.

Remember that improving self-esteem and getting comfortable with what you see in the mirror is not something to do merely once and be done with. Growing in self-love, like growing in any relationship, is an ongoing process. In fact, checking in with yourself on a daily basis is something you will be more comfortable doing the better you feel about yourself.

If you say, "Oh yuck!" when you see your face in the mirror, answer that statement with something like:

"That is not true. That is an old message."

"I do not deserve verbal abuse. I am a worthwhile person."

"Enough! I look good today. I deserve to hear it and know it."

Perceptions

Self-esteem depends greatly on self-definition or self-perception. In the Bible it says, "As a man thinketh in his heart, so is he."

On one hand, this is true. If I say I'm having an experience, then I am. I am the only one who really knows my experience. Self-definition is important as I determine choices in relationships, boundaries, desires, needs and so on.

It can also help to remember this: "I am always more than I would perceive." If you feel rotten about yourself, there is more to who you are than your mere perception.

The trick is to learn to listen to your intuition, your inner voice. You probably know in your body when you're saying something that is true, and when it's a facade. Sometimes it takes time to get to know those signals the body gives about when something doesn't feel right.

You can know by your physical reactions when your self-definition is your real experience, or when it's something you're saying from a place of fear:

- racing adrenaline
- sweaty palms
- headache
- butterflies in your stomach
- other

_____

_____

Getting to know these messages is a process of learning to use and pay attention to your body. You use "muscle memory" all the time. Your body depends on muscle memory as you are able to take for granted your ability to function day after day. Your emotional and mental muscles give you signals that become a part of your memory, a part of your integrated way of functioning.

As you learn to trust your inner voice, you know in certain moments that there is more to who you are than your fear. You learn to know that there is a balance between success and mistakes, between grandiosity and self-confidence.

Real And Ideal

Your real self is who and how you really are. It is the place where you are both okay and not okay. It is the place where you have made success and made mistakes.

Your ideal self is what you think you should be, or what you have needed to believe you are or were in order to feel okay:

- perfection
- always loving
- always nice
- always happy
- always helpful
- always well
- always sexually desirable and responsive
- always neat, organized and orderly
- always well-groomed or wonderful looking
- always needed or wanted

When you look in the mirror and are in any way tempted to say, "Yuck!" ask yourself what you believe you are supposed to be in order to pass as an okay person.

Look back at the list of qualities you just reviewed about who you should be in an ideal sense. Where are you with those qualities in a real sense on a scale from 1 (high) to 5 (low)?

Now list some adjectives in the two columns below:

I Should Be:	I Am:
Some examples are:	
perfect	fallible
always loving	often kind and loving
always nice	sometimes moody
considerate	sometimes selfish and so on.

I Am An Adult

Transactional analysis tells us that within each of us we have three ego states: parent, adult and child. This means that we emulate what we have learned about the roles of parents, adults and children in the context of our lives today.

But whether or not you are in touch with these separate components of yourself, one very important reality is that today you are an adult. What does that mean in terms of how you live your life? Let's look at responsibilities, rights and self-definition.

What responsibilities are part of being an adult for you today?

Functional (going to work, taking care of the house):

_____

_____

_____

Emotional (being attentively focused toward others, recognizing my own feelings):

_____

_____

_____

Other:

_____

_____

_____

As adults we can never go back and fill in the old pieces, but we can creatively get some of the pieces that were missing.

Are there any rights that you could not claim as a child?

- the right to an opinion
- the right to express yourself
- the right to make your own decisions
- the right to choose people with whom you spent time or were affectionate
- Other:

_____

_____

What rights did you want to have as a child that you now have today as an adult?

_____

_____

_____

What rights do you wish you had as an adult that you still feel you don't have?

- the right to be taken seriously
- the right to privacy
- the right to my own opinion
- the right not to be abandoned
- Other:

What does being an adult mean to you today?

Do you like being an adult?

What is your age today?

How comfortable are you with that age as you write it?

How do you feel about growing older?

What do you think of as you think of your elderly parents? Parents who are dead? Parents who are ill?

Expectations

What did you learn to believe from the messages your parents gave you?

The world is a friendly place.

It's a jungle out there.

You have to watch out for "those people."

Life gets better as you grow older.

Look forward to the "golden years."

Everyone is good at heart.

It's wise to give people the benefit of the doubt.

"The meek shall inherit the earth."

There is a purpose for me in the world.

I can grow and learn many things.

I am wanted, my birth was not a mistake.

I was a mistake.

I am in the way.

As you watch your parents grow older, or think of them in their later years, what do you notice happening in your beliefs?

Did life turn out for them as they told you it would for you?

Did your parents find life rewarding in later years?

What did you expect would happen to them?

What are you imagining will happen to you when you are old?

What fears do you have?

_____

_____

Anger

Apart from individual relationships, self-esteem can be strengthened by assessing how you express your emotions and how you would like to express them.

How do you handle your anger today?

    I stuff it!

    I let it fly hither and yon.

    I calculate and carefully plan my response.

    I write about it.

    I eat a lot.

    I do the laundry or house cleaning.

    I go shopping.

    I gossip.

    I throw and/or break things.

    I say things I later regret.

    I cry a lot.

    I scream and yell.

    I drive fast!

    Other:

_____

_____

I'm increasingly convinced that anger is best used as creative energy for bringing about positive change, but is not useful when merely vented. "Clearing the air" is not accomplished by verbal abuse of any kind. The one who vents the anger may feel better, but the residue will linger in the air and will be felt by those who have received the attack.

Our self-help books and teachers would remind us that we can choose or not choose to be affected by the words of others. But the truth is that not one of us lives on an island where we are immune to the energies of others. While we can make choices, we are always affected by the words we hear and the actions of others.

If this is true, what are the best ways to handle anger so that it works for us? If your anger works for, and not against you, then you can be for — and not against — giving.

Sarcasm can be fun and exciting at the moment. To come up with a quick-witted answer in the nick of time while thinking on your feet is exhilarating. But it is also hurtful. One way to handle sarcasm is to turn it into future comedy material.

Imagine a giant blackboard where you can write all of the quick-witted things you can think of. Perhaps you would draw cartoons. How are people dressed or depicted? What are they saying? What do you want to say to them?

You need to use anger, to release it so that it can work for you, but it can also be fun.

Once you have channeled your anger into some constructive or creative outlet, you are free to move on with your own personal power in a way that will allow you to have your integrity and strive toward greater community with others.

Self-Pity

We can't leave the subject of how we relate with ourselves without some discussion of how we look at and deal with self-pity.

Self-pity is condemned as one of the no-nos of recovery. It is assumed to be a destructive behavior. People certainly tire of hearing someone constantly complain. Also, many of us have a warning bell go off inside when we have endured as much self-created pain as we can handle.

So, from a practical standpoint, self-pity is not always in our best interest. Yet it exists. Honestly now, when was the last time you can remember feeling sorry for yourself? Was it just a few moments ago? This morning? Yesterday? And how do you feel being asked this question? Ashamed? Defensive? Tempted to lie?

I maintain that self-pity has the potential to be one of your best friends. It is a window to your self-worth.

When was the last time a friend of yours was struggling with something that seemed unfair? Can you remember feeling sad, wishing life would deal him or her a better hand?

Contrary to some of the vagueness of personal growth, it's still a healthy and wonderful thing to care about the well-being of others. It doesn't mean you're attempting to live their lives for them, unless you meddle against their best interests.

What if it is you who is feeling shortchanged by life?

"Get off your pity pot."

"There's always someone worse off than you."

"Count your blessings for a change."

"Build a gratitude list."

"Stop thinking of yourself and do things for others."
"Stop crying or I'll give you something to cry about."
Do these sound familiar? What comes to mind as you read them?
Memories?
Do you find yourself laughing with recognition?
Are you angry as you read them?
When was the last time you heard any of these statements said to you?

_____

When was the last time you uttered one of these statements in response to

yourself? _____

When was the last time you uttered one of these statements in response to

someone else? _____

_____

What's most important here is balance. Of course there are times when it is advantageous to put self aside and think of someone else. There are moments when a change of scenery, activity or an external focus helps to break a pattern.

But all too often we put ourselves and others down when we don't know what else to say. If there isn't time or energy to hear someone say what they've already said many times before, it may feel like self-preservation just to tell them to stop feeling sorry for themselves.

As with all punishment, it is well to look closely at our behavior and ask if the punishment we give ourselves or others is for anyone's actual good or is merely to relieve anger and frustration.

Can you remember the last time anyone told you not to be yourself? Basically, when we tell others to stop feeling or being a certain way, that is often the message that comes through. With the right rapport and the right timing, so much more is possible. With trust you can choose to take a suggestion and let it work for you in a positive way. Otherwise, you are most likely left with the task of sorting through shame in order once again to find your self-esteem.

To admit you don't have enough does not indicate you don't deserve it.

Now look at some of the needs and desires you've identified and fill in these sentences:

I deserve _____.

I need more _____

_____ in my life.

I really want _____ and want it from _____ (name).

I need _____ hugs a day.

I need to hear _____ every day.

I need time alone _____

(specify how much and how often) _____.

I need a balance between work and play _____

(specify how much time you need a day for each) _____.

We're not talking about hedonism here, although I see nothing shameful about wanting as much pleasure as possible in life. In fact, I encourage people to learn to "spoil" themselves. That word "spoil" has a rotten connotation. It deserves it when we're talking about neglected food. Perhaps it deserves it even when we're talking about neglected children. But when we're talking about enjoying pleasures, I'm afraid it has an undeserved bad reputation.

Remember: We're talking about balance.

When this friend who has been shortchanged gets out of balance, how do you feel?

When they eat too much junk food?

Stay out too late?

Violate their own boundaries?

Violate the boundaries of someone else?

Live irresponsibly?

Whatever that feeling is that you have when someone you care about is running amok, you can use that as a window to learn about yourself.

"I get angry when a friend screws up because they should know better."

"I feel taken advantage of when my friends don't take care of themselves."

"I am concerned."

If you are concerned, then that quality can be applied to how you use self-pity. You can take that concern and channel it into positive activity that will enhance your well-being.

If you are angry, then perhaps it reflects how hard you tend to be on yourself.

We need to think about the ways we punish ourselves or others.

Is the punishment really for learning and redemption, or is it a release of someone's anger and frustration?

What can you do for yourself today? What is one thing you've been putting off? What is one thing that would be a treat? What can you tell yourself that you need to hear?

"I'm okay as I am."

"I've done the best I could."

"I forgive myself."

"I love myself."

"If I were looking for someone to date, I'd pick someone just like me."

"It's okay to learn and grow and make mistakes."

"It's okay to be successful."

"I can have lots of power and esteem and still be vulnerable."

"I can be self-sufficient and still need help from others."

These statements encourage self-love, which empowers us to experience a balance between action and inner peace. To know that you can be powerful, successful, and vulnerable, all at the same time, means comprehending your worthiness.

Feelings of self-pity are signals. It is important to pay attention to them.

Wanting Perfection Equals Wanting Protection

Perfectionism is also a signal. Society has typically admired perfectionism. I can remember being told in college that when you apply for a job, it's good to be willing to say that you have weaknesses. But if you mention weaknesses like perfectionism, overworking and the like, your prospective employer will still be impressed.

But in therapy — I felt ashamed whenever anyone pointed out my striving for "perfectionism."

When was the last time you felt gripped by the curse of perfectionism?

I should have done . . . said . . . not done . . .

I should have not been me . . . I'm never good enough.

I'm stupid . . . inadequate . . . incompetent . . .

Perfectionism is a window to fear. Why would there be a reason for feelings of perfectionism if there weren't fear?

I want to be perfect, good enough, because of what someone will or will not think of me.

I want to be perfect because if and when I'm not, I'm criticized, disapproved of, put down, rejected.

If I'm not perfect:

I will lose my reputation.

I will be humiliated.

I will be punished.

I will be abandoned.

I will be invisible.

So rather than dealing with feelings of shame about perfectionism, we need to deal with the fear. Remembering it is fear and not merely perfectionism can help get to the heart of the vulnerability.

Chastising someone for perfectionistic thinking or behavior feeds shame and fear.

"Ah! If only I could get into perfectionism so perfectly that no one would catch me at it and criticize me!"

But others do see, and they usually long for equal footing so they too can express vulnerability.

But then there is also the importance of your own self-definition. Are people calling you perfectionistic because they're uncomfortable with your achieving beyond what they can handle? Or beyond what they will allow from within themselves? Or are they commenting on your perfectionism because they're closely attuned to you and can see you struggling with performance anxiety?

One way out is through not doing. What can you live with as you let some things move to lower standards? As you loosen the grip of perfectionism, some things will surely slip below your previously defined standards.

"What's the worst thing that can happen?"

Try asking yourself this question for every outcome you can imagine.

"I might lose my job!"

"And what's the worst thing that could happen if you did?"

"I'd be lost . . . I'd have to find another job . . . I'd feel like a failure . . . I'd let down my family . . ."

"And what's the worst thing about all that?"

"I'd have to start all over again!"

Usually it is catastrophic fears that keep us running after grandiose expectations. In the face of inconvenience, most of us know we would and could survive. We've already proven it time and time again. Haven't we?

Beyond the catastrophic fears are small, step-by-step challenges that ask for our concrete day-to-day attention. Self-esteem need not be threatened in the face of seeming defeat. Circumstances that have not matched our expectations may have little or nothing to do with you or me. We may be invited to act in the future with more confidence, determination or flexibility to avoid disappointment; our goals and efforts are separate from catastrophic fears that drive us into perfectionism.

Self-Forgiveness

So often when we talk about forgiveness, we refer to the forgiveness of other people. Let's remember here the importance of self-forgiveness.

I remember a nun once saying she had heard that it's up to us to forgive ourselves, and up to God to forgive everyone else.

How much lighter it makes our burden! We don't need to decide whether others "deserve" our forgiveness, are worthy and so on.

Instead, we can leave those decisions alone and merely concentrate on our own self-acceptance and forgiveness.

"But what if I'm angry?" you may be saying. "What if what someone did is unforgivable?" Then so be it. You have a right to your anger, to your perception of reality. If it is so in your experience, then it is valid. But the healing you deserve and require will come as you free yourself from the power and control of others.

I do not believe that forcing ourselves to forgive others makes any sense. Have you ever successfully forced yourself to like anything?

But from a deep place of self-forgiveness and inner peace might come an almost magical phenomenon.

On a really good day, when you feel light, whole and at one with yourself, imagine leaving that scene and delving into a backlog of resentments. Decide that now it is time to take roll call and make sure that every one of those wrongdoings are still present in your memory. You will have to leave all of the components of your good time on this wonderful day to undertake this task.

Are you eager? Are you willing?

You are probably more willing and able to count the wrongdoings of others toward you on a day when you already don't feel so peaceful and content with yourself and the world. On a good day, however, it takes more muscles to frown and conjure up the energy and the memories.

On a day when things aren't going so smoothly, and you're not so centered in a feeling of peacefulness, see if you can concentrate more on forgiveness of yourself.

Here are some questions for the struggle with self-forgiveness:

What have you done that feels especially difficult to forgive? List items if you need to, or go ahead and write pages if you need to.

Now take one thing you've done that bothers you.

What was it that you did? Be specific. _____

_____

What's the worst thing about what you did? _____

_____

If you had it to do over again, what would you like to have done instead?

_____

_____

Behind what you did is a vulnerable child with some notions about what you did. What does this child have to say? Listen some more: A wise person or a nurturing parent, a higher power also may have something to say.

Chances are, you did the best you could in the moment. If it's a mistake you've repeatedly made, then you've probably continued to do your best and perhaps can benefit from some help to get unstuck.

Confession — The Fifth Step

If we think of confession from a place of shame, then it can feel like we've relegated ourselves to a lower position in order to turn our lives around in a more positive direction.

Often people who enter 12-Step recovery are in a hurry to jump right into the Fourth and Fifth Steps. The guilt is often strong, and underneath that guilt lies tremendous feelings of shame and low self-esteem. They feel, "I could've been more . . . I should've done more." So it appears that the answer must be in taking inventory and admitting our wrongdoings. If we remember that we take our steps and various actions for the sake of healing and not for the sake of punishment, we are on a different road than the one that merely reenacts abusive patterns.

I personally used a Fifth Step once to be able to articulate "what happened." Being able to state what has happened in our lives is a major step to untangling the old and building the new. It is major to recovering our lost self-esteem.

Humility merely means remaining teachable, open to learning in a child-like way. It does not mean giving up self-esteem.

The healing of the Fifth Step or any sort of confession comes from telling another person "what happened."

What happened to you?

What was your experience? Tell a story of your life, your experience from your point of view. It's valid. You're valid. Who do you want to know and understand you? Who is someone you admire and would like to trust? This can be a person you may choose to reach out to. It may be a Fifth Step, or it may also be a way you work toward intimacy as part of your daily life toward greater freedom through self-forgiveness.

Trust the process of merely saying what happened. Allow the healing that can come as you lighten the burden of carrying secrets or hiding in isolation.

You may experience freedom from the acceptance this other person gives you. Chances are, however, that you will experience freedom through the very process of verbalizing and releasing any emotion. You will probably gain freedom from no longer carrying the feelings you've had in silence.

And as you move on in self-forgiveness, you are building a foundation for self-esteem that is solid, not disjointed. It is a foundation that allows you to feel whole, because your experience is not scattered and fragmented. You are more complete within yourself as you find self-forgiveness in a nondefensive way.

Self-forgiveness is not something that only needs to be done once and for all. It is an ongoing process that invites attention every day.

Welcome to the school of life.

PART II

Student/Teacher/Student

"Life is a metaphor for group therapy." If you can appreciate this thought, then it will come as no surprise that a primary purpose of relationships is what we can teach and learn from one another.

"But I got my self-esteem together in the last section! Isn't it enough just to work on myself?"

There are those who postulate: "No one can hurt you unless you let them." If you are the stage director of your life, this is probably true. We make choices about what we want and don't want in our daily lives. On a good day, for example, I can decide not to let a sarcastic remark from my boss ruin my day. I can decide not to let the traffic, the weather or a run in my stockings ruin my day. But if you are living your life, you aren't always directing.

Living is about being vulnerable. It's about being at the center of your experience. So how can you live at center stage of your experience and simultaneously stay in the wings rehearsing?

To always be at rehearsal or giving stage directions means being outside, away from the experience of living, guarded and not spontaneous. If you expect to be alert enough to give permission or approval before anyone ever affects you, then where will you be when it's time to simply enjoy?

To contend that "No one can hurt you unless you let them," is an oversimplification. None of us live alone on an island. We are affected by other people: what they say and don't say to us, what they do and don't do, both directly and indirectly. Other people remind us of things that happened in the past. Both the people and the memories we contact allow us to continually confront unresolved issues.

Mirror, mirror in every person! We find mirrors that give us clues and cues about ourselves and our experience. They invite us to wake up and become more fully conscious. They invite us to move beyond our present sense of ourselves, where we can experience freedom from shame and poor self-esteem. We move into synergy where we experience our power in true community with others.

Being At The Center

If you're not going to rehearse or stage direct, what does being at the center of relationships mean? It means learning from what works and what doesn't. It means being awake to your experience so you can make choices that are truly best for you.

Being at the center of your relationships means you're not guarded, nor are you a slave to the whims and wishes of others. In order not to be at the mercy of others, you need to be in charge of your life. That means you need to know and to express yourself, to be able to make choices about what works best and who you want to relate "with."

The Sorting Process

Remember: This process of personal growth is for bringing about increased joy, not just for the mere sake of "working" or "learning." So why not start by looking at some positives? Finding out where you are comfortable and with whom will serve as valuable contrast as you also grow in recognition of those things that do not work in your life.

Who Do You Like?

Have you ever thought about who you like and who you don't like? Have you considered that you have a right to make those kinds of distinctions and choices, that you don't have to take whatever comes along and assume a role you don't want to carry out? Some people choose their friends based on proximity and convenience. Some marvelous gifts and lessons can come with proximity, and others can come about with clear choices.

How Do You Know Who You Like?

We're often not encouraged to consider who we do and don't like. Instead, we're often expected to "like":

- those who are "nice" to us
- those who are friendly
- those in proximity to us.

We often want to avoid conflict and so passively go for a ride in a relationship without considering what we really want. Some relationships get to be like old shoes. They become comfortable out of familiarity. After all, they're stretched out, broken in; they're safe and secure in a way.

But what about those shoes that really fit, that you know you like? How do you know they fit? And how do you know you really like them? Do they fit because you don't get or expect much support from them, and therefore you can just quickly slip in and out of them? Do they fit because you like their color and style, and by God you're going to make them fit? Do they fit because they feel good? Can you feel proud in them? Did you think you could never fit into them?

Who are some people you know you like? Name three.

_____

_____

_____

What are some specific things you like about them?

_____

_____

_____

What do you like . . .

- about the way they look?
- about the way they sound?
- about the way they touch?
- about the way they smell?

What do you like about your best friend?

- appearance
- smell
- voice
- smile
- touch
- presence
- way of listening

- laugh
- moods
- expressiveness
- Other:

_____

_____

What behaviors has this person displayed that you've liked?

_____

_____

What values have you seen this person display that you like?

_____

_____

What do you like about your lover or a past lover?
    appearance
    smell
    voice
    smile
    touch
    presence
    way of listening
    laugh
    moods
    expressiveness
    Other:

_____

_____

What behaviors has this person displayed that you've liked?

_____

_____

What values have you seen this person display that you like?

_____

_____

What do you like about your boss?
    appearance
    smell
    voice

smile
touch
presence
way of listening
laugh
moods
expressiveness
Other:

_____

_____

What behaviors has your boss displayed that you've liked?

_____

_____

What values have you seen your boss display that you like?

_____

_____

Think of an acquaintance you've met recently, whom you liked.
What did you notice liking about this person?
appearance
smell
voice
smile
touch
presence
way of listening
laugh
moods
expressiveness
Other:

_____

_____

What behaviors has this person displayed that you've liked? _____

_____

What values have you seen this person display that you like? _____

_____

How Do You Know When You Don't Like Someone?

Sometimes we learn what we want by going through what we don't want. You may know more about yourself from noticing what and whom you like, but you probably know even more about yourself by noticing what and whom you don't like.

What do you notice in your body when you don't like someone? What does your neck feel like? What does your stomach feel like? What do your hands feel like? What happens to your breathing?

How do you feel when you notice what's going on in your body?

tired
fidgety
sick
nervous
angry
depressed
Other:

_____

_____

How do you behave?

I act friendly.
I withdraw.
I chatter.
I find a way to get away.
I become sarcastic.
I use humor.
I eat more.
I eat less.
I drink.
I use sex.
I get revenge.
Other:

_____

_____

Is there a difference between how you feel and how you behave?

Do you act one way to cover or protect how you really feel?

The point here is to know for yourself what clues and cues are available to help you know when you like someone. There is a myth that says we should like or love everyone equally. Can you remember ever trying to do that, hoping others such as parents would do that for you? It's an old notion about being "fair" that assumes that we can like or love everyone the same, and then no one will ever be left out; no one will ever be hurt.

You can learn to like and love people for different reasons and in various ways. Thus, you can give yourself even more room to make a variety of choices about how you will respond to people, based upon the choices you make about relationships.

I remember one time when I was very upset about a grade I had received. It was not uncommon for teachers and graduate students to socialize with one another, and this teacher and I were beginning to become friends. We had discussed having lunch together. When I told my therapist how upset I was about the grade I had received, she asked, "Is this teacher someone you want just as a teacher, or is she also someone you want as a friend?" I immediately knew she was someone I wanted only as a teacher. "Well then," said my therapist, "your response in this situation is very different than if you wanted her as a friend."

This was a first lesson for me about "different" kinds of relationships. Some people in the human potential movement encourage us to treat everyone the same, to feel the same about everyone. It is freeing to know that indeed we have choices. We have "different" reactions and feelings about "different" people in the world; therefore why not have different choices about how we relate? A box of candy, a row of paintings, a field of flowers, a box full of puppies — all of these will contain an assortment from which to make choices. You owe it to yourself, to your growing self-esteem, to give yourself a variety of experiences in relationships. The more aware you are of your decisions, the freer you are to make choices that are clearly in line with your desires and what's best for you.

Categories Of Friends

Sometimes making choices about relationships can become clearer with a few baseline categories. You may want to use these or come up with your own. You may find that you want to categorize your feelings about people differently as you add life experiences.

Here is an example of a place you might wish to begin: Bedroom friends, living room friends and front porch friends.

Bedroom friends are people with whom you can be most vulnerable. They are people with whom you can share your private, most inward thoughts, feelings and experiences. They are the ones with whom you can "let it all hang out." It is safe to be truly honest with them.

(They may or may not be people with whom you have sex. When I first came up with these categories, the bedroom friends in my life were very close to me. The people I went to bed with, on the other hand, were not people with whom I could safely be vulnerable.)

Living room friends are social friends. They are nice for some companionship, for sharing ideas, perhaps working on hobbies or projects, and perhaps for knowing some of the more peripheral details of your life. You may want to "hang out" with them, but may not choose to share with them when the chips are down or when you want to tell someone what your dreams in life really are.

Front porch friends are acquaintances. They are nice to say hello to, but not folks you want to have on the inside of your private or social life. It may be okay to borrow something, to chit-chat, to laugh with them, to exchange information. But you wouldn't necessarily think of inviting them to dinner or to move in with you.

I've found enormous freedom by using this system to gain clarity.

Nothing is written in stone. As with folders in a filing cabinet, friendships can be portable or removable.

These categories allow you to decide your choices based on your own needs and feelings, without having to take inventory of anyone else. You don't need to justify your feelings by analyzing anyone else's behavior or lifestyle. You only need to make your choices. By listening to your desires and your needs based on your response to categories such as these, you are allowing your own integrity to grow by taking responsibility for choosing and setting your own personal boundaries.

We don't have enough time or energy to have an intimate relationship with everyone we know. Some of us have been so glad to discover the joy of honest communication that we think we should be able to communicate with everyone that way all of the time.

Now seriously, do you really want to hear all of the emotional reactions and disclosures of every person with whom you interact?

A major key here is self-honesty, making choices. The intimacy you find with those you truly like will be more intense if you don't try to be so totally open or disclosing with everyone.

Consider, too, your own time and energy. How much time do you spend maintaining close friendships or other intimate relationships? How much time do you need to spend?

    Each day
    each week
    each month
    through each year.

Do you plan how you will spend time and energy building relationships?

What are some things you want to be able to talk about? With whom?

_____

_____

What are some ways you want to spend time with intimate people in your life?

    sitting and talking
    spending quiet time together
    listening to music
    going to the beach
    going for a walk
    going to a movie
    going for counseling
    going to church
    going to a meeting
    Other:

_____

It's difficult to find enough time or energy to have intimate relationships with everyone. There are only 24 hours in a day.

But how often have you lost sleep over the people you didn't really notice, all those people who you pass by day after day and never know much about? Not much.

Likewise, do you really think that other people lose sleep over your choices about friendships?

Many of us have lost sleep when we knew we were not being honest with ourselves about what was truly right for us.

    Trusting the wrong person with something that you want kept private.
    Displaying more loyalty to someone else than you give to yourself.
    Allowing yourself to be violated in any way.
    Betraying a confidential remark.

The guilt we feel from these mistakes can be a real friend, like the "still small voice within." It is letting us know when we have "missed the mark," been less than our best. We don't have to think of ourselves in big trouble, we only need to be willing to turn our behavior around so that in future situations we behave differently.

"But I don't want to make a mistake!"

How often have you stayed in a relationship because you didn't want to admit that you . . .

    changed your mind?
    misjudged someone?
    are a different person now than when you first made that decision?

That loyalty you've displayed is often so strong that you feel foolish admitting that perhaps you've changed your mind.

That Urgent Feeling

What about those times when you're obsessed with someone?

"I can't stop thinking about . . ."

"I've never felt so wonderful now that I've met . . . I think of . . ."

"I've never hated anyone so much!"

"This person has ruined my life and I can't stop thinking about how much I hate him/her!"

Are these extremes related? Chances are, those feelings of urgency can tell us much about ourselves.

Our fantasies, scripts, internal dramas can come to the surface if we are willing to look beyond our mere reactions.

What does this person remind you of?

A dream? A drama? A time when you hoped you would get your needs met and were abandoned instead? A time when you were mistreated, short-changed, abused?

Are you reliving that dream or that drama once again?

When we allow someone to dictate our time and energy by becoming obsessed with thoughts about that person, we are making that person the barometer for our self-esteem. Here is how some of my clients have described it:

"It's like being addicted to someone, a high, then a letdown — as in a hangover." "Feeling like a yo-yo, going up and down by how that other person feels, behaves, talk and acts." In other words, you've let that person take your power. What can you learn about yourself so that you get your power back? Ask yourself some questions:

Is this feeling similar to something you've felt before?

What do you wish this person would do or not do?

Does this remind you of another time in your life when you wanted something similar to change?

What is remaining unfinished about that earlier time?

Is there something you wish you could have said?

Is there something you've yet to be able to ask for?

Is there something you need or want that you've been hoping someone else would figure out?

Sometimes we think, "If this person would read my mind and give me what I want, then I'd know I'm worthwhile." But that's a fantasy. As we more fully take up our power of making choices, we find that other people also make choices, that they are not passive to the expression of our wants and needs.

By taking responsibility for our experience, we can feel more whole, and less likely to be tossed about by the reactions of others.

But personal growth is about changing our minds. We make mistakes. Sometimes we use each other like scrap paper, making our marks, then discarding what we don't need after we have learned.

When I think about the people I like, I . . .

    look forward to seeing them
    feel warm inside
    feel a sense of joy
    am clear about their place in my life.

Some Subtle Things To Ask Yourself

Do I like those whom others tell me they like?
Do I like others based on who likes me?
Do I like those who do favors for me, who I see every day?
Do I like people who are less fortunate than I, who are perhaps safe?
Do I like people who are successful in my eyes?
Do I like people who are vulnerable in ways similar to me?

"Courage To Change The Things I Can"

Is there anyone whom you've been putting at a higher place in your life than you have really wanted? Is there someone you would like to recognize as a closer person?

What are some little things you can change?

_____

_____

_____

_____

Is there a big change that needs to be made?
What do you need in order to start or add to the process of change?

_____

_____

_____

_____

What support do you have?

_____

_____

What support do you need?

_____

_____

What fear do you have?

_____

_____

If you let go of something that is not good or right for you, or make a change in your life, what do you imagine will happen with the empty space that's left?

_____

_____

_____

What would you like to do with that space? Here is room for some of your own responses.

_____

_____

_____

And so we make choices, decisions. We use our past experience to help us decide what our direction will be by noticing what has worked and what has not. We take pieces from our past that add to or subtract from our lives today. What are some pieces that you can bring with you that will continue adding to your self-esteem?

Memories

What are some of the things people did for you as a child that are your treasured memories?

I remember my sister and my mother reading to me, not just once or twice, but on numerous occasions. Reading to someone is a gift. It means taking time, daring to speak what you see aloud. It means giving a particular kind of attention to someone — a kind of attention that doesn't really demand anything, but says that the person listening has all of your time in this moment.

What do you remember that people did for you or gave to you?
- They listened.
- They played.
- They accepted me.
- They laughed.
- We made music.
- They gave me knowledge.
- They gave me information.
- They gave me spirit.
- They were a role model.
- They gave me permission.
- They gave me forgiveness.
- They gave me childhood.
- They were a parent.
- They were a brother or sister.
- They gave me friendship.
- They wanted my opinions, thoughts and feelings.
- They missed me when I went away.
- They cared enough to get mad at me.
- They gave me room to be me.
- Other:

_____

_____

In what ways do you continue to treasure pieces of those memories in your life today? Perhaps some of the ways you can enjoy closeness might have to do with finding pieces of those memories in new ways.

Pieces I still carry:

_____

_____

_____

Who did you get these pieces from?

_____

_____

_____

How are these pieces helpful today?

_____

_____

Who in your present life reminds you of or rebuilds those pieces?

_____

_____

_____

You will not find anyone who will completely fill either your old memories or any loss you've known, but this doesn't mean you have to throw your memories away.

How do you feel when you remember some of the things people have done with and for you?

What do you think of, and how do you feel when you remember them?

Where are those relationships now?

Is there anything you would like to say to those people?

_____

_____

_____

Can you? _____

Will you? _____

_____

Is there anything you can say to people in your life today that you learned from those relationships?

_____

_____

_____

Cherish your memories. Let them work for you as they add continuity, clarity and nourishment to your sense of self.

Is This Person In My Life?

Do I want this person in my life?

Yes.

Maybe.

No way!

Again, these are decisions based on your needs and not about anyone else's worth, rights or lifestyle. You're not deciding whether someone has the right to live a quality life. You're simply deciding where, if at all, you want them in your life. This includes — and may not necessarily exclude — family. You may feel that members of your family are bedroom friends, or you may feel that family practice "demands" that they at least be a part of your living room.

You can ask yourself these questions about any and every relationship. Don't assume that just because someone is playing the part of a bedroom friend, that it is where you really want them. On the other hand, someone who has been a front porch friend for years might really be someone you want as a bedroom friend.

Once you decide where you want various people in your life, you can choose a way to communicate with them that reflects the type of relationship you want.

Communication

Some people think that the way to communicate with everyone is to be "open" and "honest." But jargon like that gets thick, boring and old as some of us begin to wonder where the person behind all that talk really is. With an expectation to be so open, you are bound to be disappointed. We have neither the time nor the energy to be open with everyone. If everyone in turn was so honest with you, you would not have time to accomplish anything or to live your life.

Besides, if we all communicated the same way, or with the same intensity, on what basis would you make choices about where and with whom to be intimate?

The place to begin with communication is with yourself. It may not be important to the bus driver, to your boss or to the store clerk that you felt violated when they did something. The relationship you have with a distant neighbor may not warrant your blastings about sexist language, and how you felt discriminated against by their choice of words. It depends upon what you really want. Do you want them to know how you feel, regardless of what the relationship is? Is it worth the time and energy it will take to say your piece and deal with the aftermath? What are some possible consequences?

Whether or not you decide to tell them your reaction, it's most important that you let yourself know. Knowing, for instance, that you are offended when someone uses a particular tone, is great information to have when choosing where you want certain relationships or types of people to be in your life. It may not be worth your time and energy to tell a store clerk how you feel when you receive a patronizing tone, but it may be worthwhile to tell a close friend if you suddenly feel a change in her attitude toward you, or if you have long held such a personal reaction in secret.

Sharing your reactions with those you choose carefully allows you to have time and energy left for living your life. After all, that is what all this personal growth jazz is about.

So how do you behave when you let go of some people? How do you treat them and yourself with respect, knowing that you choose not to be so open and honest with them? Perhaps answering some questions will help.

What are safe areas of conversation? What do you have in common (sports, work, cooking and so on)?

What do you like about this person?

What do you actually need, right now, from this person (a ticket to a movie, your food in a restaurant, an item in a particular store and so on)?

Not everything we need is emotionally laden. If we can accept that most people will not have anything to do with our self-esteem, we can more easily take charge of the ways in which we do see that we are nurtured and nourished.

Okay. So you've decided to let go of some of the people you don't have an intimate relationship with, you've learned to let your personal reactions serve as valuable information. How about those relationships where you choose to be intimate? How do you communicate? And how do you find or maintain your self-esteem?

Remember, you've made choices. To carry these choices to fruition takes commitment.

Commitment means responsible actions to support choices.

Commitment means you have made a decision. You may not have made a commitment to report your honest feelings to your living room or front porch friends, to store clerks and bus drivers who are not a part of your personal life, but your close relationships need and deserve the care of your commitment in order to remain active as bedroom friends.

Assuming you know who the people are who you want as bedroom friends — which can be a lifelong lesson and process of choice in and of itself — the task of communicating is about follow-through.

"How do I say what I mean and mean what I say?"

Have you ever wondered about those simple phrases?

The effort that you have applied in your attempts to understand a child, a pet or even a puzzle is the same earnest effort you deserve as you reach to say what you mean and mean what you say.

Your inner child deserves your fine-tuned listening, the respect that comes from listening to and through your intuition. Call it compassion, self-forgiveness, grace. You have a right and a responsibility to give this act of kindness to yourself first, then you can give it naturally and genuinely to others.

Self-Honesty:
What Do I Really Want?

If you are guarded about saying what you want to others all the time, you may not honestly know what you yourself want.

It dawned on me once that I was probably being only half honest about what I wanted — and if I was lucky, I was getting half of that. This meant that I was getting about one-fourth of what I wanted. No wonder I felt powerless in my relationships much of the time!

Now it's time to be honest with yourself. In a quiet place — through meditation, journal writing or whatever form of introspective communication you best use — ask yourself some questions to determine what it is you want right now.

What does my body need? What does my body want?

    affection (hugs, kisses, touch and so on)

    genital stimulation

    massage

    space and separateness

What does my child within want?

    to be heard

    to be understood

    to be accepted

    to play

    to reduce fear

    to get angry

    to think quietly

What does your wise person or adult within believe is good for you? What are your options? What messages do you repeatedly hear about what you should do? Who is talking from your past?

_____

_____

_____

Do you know that your body talks? It gives you messages about what you want and need. It tells you about things that are not good for you. So when you're trying to figure out what is best for you, listen to what your body is saying. It may be giving you clues about relationships, about boundaries, about who gets close and who does not, about who is fun . . .

In the first edition of *The Wellness Workbook* by John Travis, M.D., and Regina Ryan, Regina has a journal entry in which she realizes that the bulk of the word "shoulder" is "should."

Who is sitting on your shoulders, telling you what you "should do," "should be," "should not do," "should not be"? Who is there?

_____

_____

What do you want to say to them?

_____

_____

_____

As you make choices about relationships, about what works and what doesn't, the statements you make to yourself continue to be important. The tone and quality of what you keep in your own mind is your responsibility — don't leave it to what others decide to say and not say to you.

Remember, too, that relationships serve a valuable purpose. You are not off on a separate island making statements to yourself. Intimacy building can be about learning much about each other's vulnerability, joy, needs and wants as well as internal dialogue. We can gain much healing as we dare to share our personal vulnerability with one another as well as our joy.

What is intimacy with another person in its most ideal sense? Is it based on the highest level of trust imaginable? Is it a type of communion experience? Perhaps we know at some level that this is the potential of good sexual experience.

So what does it mean if you are going to bed with someone you deem as a "bedroom friend?" It means that sex is not mechanical. It is not an experience separate from vulnerable sharing. It is a place for feeling safe, close and comfortable. It is a place of trusting to "let go" and truly be affected by another person. Here is a time when we need to use all we have learned about healthy self-esteem, our own, and how we profit through our relationships. Sex challenges our self-esteem. It is messy. It carries expectations and assumptions of "performance." Society tells us what or who is desirable.

If orgasm were the only purpose to sex, there would be no reason for two people to have this experience with one another. There is more to it than the ending, the finale, the climax. There is bonding, warmth, affection and deeper levels of knowing your partner.

All this takes risk, a willingness to say what feels good and right, and what you want to be different. It means knowing your self-esteem is strong enough to listen to what your partner likes and dislikes. This is not about deciding whether you are okay as a lover; it is learning about being close and intimate.

As we continue to work on the statements we make to ourselves, and as we make choices about who the people are who give us nurturance and nourishment, we can give thought to the words we use when speaking to others.

Choosing And Using Words

Our words are important. They are similar to the clothes we wear, the food we eat, the people we choose to relate with or the surroundings we choose. They suggest, they set tone or atmosphere, they invite and add color. If we wear sloppy clothes, we attract sloppiness or a more casual response. If we choose an environment that is down to earth, we are more likely to attract such people.

The same is true regarding our choice of words. If we use words that are kind, nonjudgmental and nonintrusive, we are more likely to get a receptive response than if we use words that are sarcastic or invasive.

Beginning With Ourselves

In Part I we spent a long time on statements we make to ourselves. If we use loving communication when talking with others but still mutter negative comments to and about ourselves, our unconscious is still experiencing low self-esteem. The words we use with ourselves need to be carefully chosen.

Just as you carefully select produce from the grocery store, checking the way it feels, looks and smells before you decide to buy it, you have the same right to check out how your words feel.

If you're used to saying that you're stupid, sick or always unable to do something right, now's your chance to find a new way to talk with yourself. Instead of calling yourself stupid, you can say something like: "I have made this mistake before. I wonder what I can learn so that I don't keep making it."

As you become more selective about your own word choice, you will become more selective about what you accept that is said to you by others and, in turn, the words you choose when speaking with others. If you're going to get close to someone, what words do you need to hear that invite self-respect or the feeling of being safe enough to disclose? When we are thinking about building intimacy, it is self-defeating to use words that carry negative meaning.

What words do you use to refer to the bodies of other people?

_____

What words do you use for saying what you desire to have done to your own body?

_____

What words do you use for sexual intercourse, lovemaking or intimacy building?

_____

Some Things To Keep In Mind

When I say "you," I mean "me."

Have you ever heard someone say how "you" feel, and find yourself wondering who they're talking about? They say: "When you're in this situation or this kind of a relationship, you feel . . ." It's as though there is one way to feel in that situation and they're going to tell you what it is. It allows for a set of rigid expectations that are sure to lead to disappointment. You will not be able to live out what they assume, and they will find that most people do not live just one way (their way). It also allows the one doing the assuming to dodge being vulnerable and more personally disclosing.

When I hear someone saying a lot about "you" I often ask, "Is that how it is for you?" If they aren't willing to personalize it from my suggestion, then I ask, "Are you saying that about me?" They usually say "Oh, no, no, no! I'm just saying it in general." Or sometimes they say that they mean it for themselves.

If I say "me" or "I" instead of "you," I may feel more vulnerable but I'm really giving myself much more room. All I need to do is listen to my intuition, my own reality. I don't need to do what "should" be true for the universe, or even for myself by some sort of global expectation. It also allows others much more freedom to be able to respond without being pounced on with assumptions. If someone assumes they know what I'm feeling, I'm more likely to be defensive.

It is much less invasive to communicate with "I" statements. I may tell you how I feel about you, something you said or did, but it is clear that I am giving you my perception.

Questions And Statements

Making statements instead of asking questions leaves much more room for people to choose to share with us. A barrage of questions can be smothering and intrusive. People mean well, but often they are unsure about how and what to say, so they take the safe way out by asking questions rather than making statements. If asking a question is appropriate and is something you want to do, then ask questions that are open-ended and noninterrogating. Or ask questions when you sense that people are really participating with you in a conversation. Are they giving you complex responses? Is their tone open and friendly? Do they seem present to you and to the discussion? If so, then perhaps your questions feel like a safe and welcoming invitation. If you are only getting one-word answers, then perhaps some space is needed and another approach.

I happen to be blind. I used to assume that if I patiently answered other people's questions, there would come a day when they had asked enough and then I would be able to get on with being me, would have my turn at getting more recognition as a human being. But you know what? They never stopped asking. They never seemed to learn I was a real person. So I usually went away feeling diminished.

Questions, in the right time and within the right relationships, can be like doors. They can invite personal sharing. Questions can be a sign that you want to know more about someone or that someone else wants to know more about you. But they can also be invasive, can give you a feeling that you are cornered or that you're filling out a registration form of some kind.

Think about the questions people have asked you over the years. Has anyone ever asked you personal questions you thought were inappropriate? Perhaps you've had people pry into your personal life as if what they wanted to know was somehow their business. If your self-esteem is shaky, you may not know that it's okay not to answer, or know how to do so without showing your rage.

The flip side of learning not to ask so many questions and how to make more disclosing statements, is to learn how to say no to the questions of others:

"It's really none of your business."

"Why do you want to know?"

"I'd rather consider sharing that information with you when and if we get to know each other better."

"I don't feel like answering questions right now."

"What is this, a registration form?"

"What are you trying to say behind your question?"

Some of these statements are more abrupt than others. Some are statements that could be said with a smile and a bit of teasing. Nobody likes to be put on the spot. Which retort you use depends upon what kind of relationship you want.

Some of these statements may drive people away. Some may build a bridge upon which you can begin to build a different quality of sharing. Saying, "I don't feel like answering questions right now. But if and when we get to know each other better, I'll be happy to answer more personal questions about myself," gives people the sense that they can stay, that they can find other ways of getting comfortable with you.

Perhaps they will not be able to stop asking. Some people's interpersonal skills are limited. Making your statement about not answering questions will show you more clearly the people who can recognize you as a human being and those who cannot see beyond labels. So you end up with more information, which you can use to make your choices.

It is better to ask questions than to hold back concern or desire to know something. But there is something to be said for respecting boundaries and the process of rapport development.

So what about those times when you really do want or need to know something? Are there appropriate, nonintrusive ways to ask a question? I believe there are.

Questions can be like invitations. They can ease the awkwardness and give permission for someone to feel okay about disclosing. But these kinds of questions are best when they're open-ended, leaving room for a person to consider what he or she really wants you to know.

"What do you want or need?"

"What's going on? What's happening?"

"Is there something I can do? Is there something you want or need from me?"

While the last may be a specific question, it still empowers the person to consider his or her needs and wants, without your judgment of what those needs and wants "should" be.

Respecting Boundaries

"I grow in my ability to sensitively respect the boundaries of others as I accept the realities of my own boundaries."

This is an affirmation that I use to help set boundaries, and to relax more comfortably with the boundaries others set that may shut me out.

Thinking About Boundaries

How do you feel when people touch you? What are your reactions? Do you ever find that when some people touch you it feels good, while when others touch you, you feel violated?

These messages are important to your spirit. Respecting them will help you build true intimacy with another person.

If you merely shut down, freeze and passively condone what is going on, chances are you're not really there in the moment but have left your body to serve as a vessel.

Listening to your reactions about what feels good and what doesn't, then learning to speak up when the relationship is important enough to do so, are skills that take time to learn. They take time to build as skills and added time to build within each relationship. You will probably find that you feel more whole, more complete and fully alive as you're able to communicate this fully both to yourself and with another.

Concern Versus Worry

I believe there is a difference between concern and worry, both in behavior and effect.

If I am concerned about you, I can offer this and still give you room to make your choices. With my concern, I can recognize your integrity and let you use the muscles of your own mind and behavior to take responsibility for your own life.

If, on the other hand, I am worried, then I am not trusting you. What happens to your self-esteem if you are continuously fed the worry-energy, the doubt and mistrust of others all the time? Chances are, you'll have a more difficult time maintaining positive self-esteem.

The "Let Me Chew Your Food For You" Routine

Have you ever had people decide that you "must be" hungry, tired, thirsty, angry, sad, happy . . .? They know. If you try to tell them otherwise, they respond, "There's something wrong with you." These people feel safe, they feel that life is predictable, nonthreatening — so long as you are in your appropriate niche.

Now think about a time when you offered help and the person declined. How did you feel when you went away? Did you say, "Well, I offered. If he decides to change his mind, I'll be here." Or did you say, "I offered, and after all I've done for him that will be the last time I offer him anything! If it weren't for me, he wouldn't have had it so good!"

If you went away peacefully, without needing him to appreciate you and feed your ego, chances are you did it for him. But if you went away angry, you probably offered it more for yourself. Using other people, keeping them dependent, holding on tightly to the need to be needed is what contributes to helping professionals who are less than effective and relationships that don't work well.

Luck Or Success?

Luck implies chance. Do we want the people we care about to know they deserve the good things that happen, or do we believe that their good fortune is a mere function of chance?

I feel that the phrase "Good luck!" is another "worry" phrase. It implies a lack of trust in that person's ability to create or realize dreams and projects.

Saying No

Do you believe it's okay to say no? I find that the ability to say no is situational. Some circumstances are easier than others.

How do you know when you're comfortable saying no?

_____ I say no easily, calmly and nondefensively.

_____ I say no without having to give a list of reasons or excuses, without having to justify.

_____ I say no without having to be aggressive or unduly angry.

I'm often amazed at the behavior I see. A person who has not previously taken care of himself or herself will say no angrily and the person who hears the answer also gets a lot of aggressive force behind it. Many times people will defensively give a list of reasons why their answer is no.

Do you really want to hear a list of reasons? Usually we're in a hurry, we're busy with our own projects. No is no, and all those reasons are better left for another discussion. Hearing no means that you need to spend time and energy coming up with alternatives. Hearing others' lists of reasons, their own problems and needs, is a further drain on time and energy.

Sometimes we are tempted to give reasons because we feel guilty that we can't say yes. Sometimes we want others to know that their needs are not the only needs in the world, that other people have problems. But if we give thought to what is most effective when we are asking for favors, when indeed, we do hear no as the answer, we can keep these things in mind when we ourselves are saying no. Learning to take better care of ourselves . . . not saying yes when we do need to say no, recognizing when our bodies are saying and feeling no . . . will help a lot. We do not need to justify our reasons. We do not need to ask for permission.

Personal Time Management

Are you in charge of the decisions about how much time you spend alone and how much time you spend with others? What do you need in terms of time with others and time alone? Do you get enough?

What signals do you get that you are not getting enough time alone? What do you notice in your moods, your lifestyle, your food habits, your attitude, your spirituality?

_____

_____

_____

How about when you're not getting enough time with others? What is that like for you? Are there specific "others" you need more time with? Who are they?

_____

_____

_____

What would give your time with others more quality?
    If we talk more.
    If we talk about _____.
    If we play more.
    If we find common interests.
    If we talk less about work.
    If we enjoy more aesthetics.
    If we use our intelligence together more.
    If we share more affection.
    If we express our mutual appreciation of one another.
    Other:

_____

_____

What commitments do you have for time you spend with others? How much time do you spend each week? Each month? How much time each day, week, or month do you need alone?

    _____ minutes per __ _____

    _____ hours per _____

Do you have a favorite place for your time alone? Where is that?

_____

_____

Write a description of the place and space that you like to call your own. Can you create a space that is totally yours? What is it like?

_____

_____

_____

Managing time means clear communication with self and others. We first decide what our commitments are, then we follow through. We say no to others when it's important to have time alone, when it's important to have time with someone else or others. Saying "I need time alone" or "I need time with you" or "I want this time" doesn't have to be based on "need."

Working With Fantasies

"Fantasy is healthy."
"Fantasy is a sign of immaturity, co-dependency . . ."

Again, the truth is "balance." Too much fantasy can mean that we're missing out on life, avoiding the business and the joy of living. On the other hand, you can learn much about your needs, desires, fears and expectations by paying attention to your fantasies. Do you imagine something that happens over and over? Is there someone you keep thinking of, or a particular memory you repeatedly have? Those fantasies are clues, landmarks to what's going on within you. They are not to be shamed or buried. They are for your information. Respect them as windows.

What are your fantasies?

_____

_____

_____

What do you wish?

_____

_____

_____

Who is there?

_____

_____

What is he/she saying?

_____

_____

_____

How are you responding?

_____

_____

_____

How are you feeling?

_____

_____

_____

What fantasies do you have when you're angry?

_____

_____

What do you imagine when you're angry?

_____

_____

Who is there?

_____

What happens?

_____

_____

What are you saying?

_____

What are you doing?

_____

What is the outcome?

_____

_____

How do you feel?

_____

_____

What's important about these fantasies is not that we necessarily act them out, but rather that we not be afraid of them. If we cower from them in fear, we give them power and they continue to eat at us. If we face them, we keep them from driving us. Even the good, positive fantasies are more able to work for us when we own them. Then we can more realistically go to work to actualize goals.

Laughter And Tears

Have you ever noticed how a real hard cry sounds and even feels similar to a hearty laugh? Yet we often assume they are at opposite ends of a continuum. When we are fully expressing, our perceptions help us to determine whether we are happy, sad, laughing or crying.

Again, we're talking about balance. If I expect to laugh all the time, I will not laugh fully because I won't have allowed the healing and balance that comes from allowing tears. If I hold in sadness, then I'm spending lots of energy "holding" and cannot freely release, even joy!

Research has shown that toxins are actually released from the body when we cry. These tears are chemically different from the tears stimulated by cutting an onion. When you laugh or cry, you're freeing up your body and your emotions.

Dr. Sidney B. Simon, in his personal growth workshops, reminds us that when we cry, the healing has already begun. Dr. Annette Goodheart tells us that we don't laugh because we're happy; rather, we're happy because we laugh. We need to accept that we have all kinds of feelings, and releasing and expressing them is part of the process of living. We expect ourselves to get rid of body waste. Why not tears? We expect ourselves to be able to eat for nourishment. Why not laughter as another source of nourishment?

Things That Make Me Laugh

Can you remember the last time you laughed really hard? When was it?

_____

_____

_____

Describe some things about your laugh.
    It's loud and full.
    It's quiet and contained.
    I seldom laugh out loud.
    I laugh when other people laugh.
    I laugh freely and often.

About Crying

When was the last time you cried?

_____

_____

Can you remember a time when you cried from the depths of your being?

Describe how you cry.

   _____ I never cry.

   _____ I cry only when alone.

   _____ I don't make any noise when I cry.

   _____ I cry often.

   _____ I sob.

   _____ I get a headache.

   _____ I feel ashamed when I cry.

   _____ I feel better when I cry.

To Hug, Or Not To Hug?

Hugs are great! Many of us often feel as if we don't get enough. And some of us also feel as if we don't want to be under pressure to do so. The pressure to hug is like the old pressure to "be nice," or any other old form of "programmed" social behavior you can think of, it just has a different face.

I encourage you to get what you need. If you find in certain times that you need or want more hugs, then think about who you want them from, where and how. Do you want your whole body hugged? Do you want to just hug from the shoulders up? There may be different hugs for different times, people and relationships.

When you don't want to hug certain people, then give yourself permission to set up a "Say no to hugs" campaign. It is risky to say no, particularly when the other person assumes hugging you is okay. If someone's going to be assertive enough to touch you without your permission, then you have a right to say no without asking permission.

Holding Versus Hugging

There's quite a difference between hugging and holding, between being hugged and being held. When we hug, we're usually still on our feet, on guard, ready for what's coming "next." When we're held, we can choose to let go, unload, trust that it's okay.

In our society only children and people engaged in a sexual experience have permission to be held. We are saying that a person has to be childlike or sexual to get held, or to have the closeness that allows for the openness of being held.

In this context hugging has become an acceptable compromise, but it is just that. Holding and being held is where much real bonding, trusting and deep communing with another person take place.

You don't have to be sexual to get held. Lots of people who report struggling with sexual addiction say it goes back to sexual abuse issues in their lives, or a deep need for a way to get the affection and comfort they've craved. You don't have to be sick to get held. Hospitals are filled with people who get more touching in those settings than they do in any other part of their lives.

And you don't have to be a child to get held. You don't have to act like a child, act out sexual games, talk baby talk, be helpless or give up personal power of any kind to deserve getting the quality intimacy you seek.

Naming Your Own Bottom Line

It takes lots of courage, but there is much to be said for naming your own bottom line: What will you do? What won't you do? What will you tolerate?

I will be friendly.

I won't engage in genital behavior with you.

I will spend half an hour with you.

I will call you three times and no more without a response from you.

Using "And" Instead Of "But"

"I will spend half an hour with you 'and' we will see where our friendship goes with time."

"I will spend half an hour with you 'but' we will see where our friendship goes with time."

Do you notice a difference between these two sentences? The first is positive, open-ended. The second is negative. The second half of the sentence negates the first half, implying that there is doubt about the friendship. The 'and' sentence does not imply that you are any more certain about where the friendship will go; it simply leaves more room for various possible outcomes.

Taking Time Out

There's a lot to be said for the healing that can come from taking time out from the intensity of a relationship. Sometimes just putting something on hold for a few days or a few hours can remove the urgency long enough to approach the present situation with a fresh perspective.

Abandonment

I've thought about doing a workshop and calling it: "When Will My Abandonment Issues Abandon Me?" If abandonment is one of your core issues, then it is one of your life projects to grow through. Taking time out from the intensity of a relationship may be an ambivalent task, one you feel you need and dread simultaneously. Knowing this is the case can help remove the low self-esteem scenarios from your thoughts when you are trying to create healthy distance.

If I know that abandonment is one of my issues, then I don't have to get upset about someone else's distance. I can deal with my own grief responsibly. It's not less painful, but can be less complicated.

Time

How much time is good for you to spend with people? Part of boundary setting is looking at how we block out our time. Deciding about larger or smaller chunks of time to spend with people is valuable when we are determining ways to stop our buttons from being pushed. Granted, we can't control all the ways our buttons get pushed — they will, in spite of our intentions and efforts. But we can plan our time, plan ways to surround ourselves with supportive and nurturing people.

So give yourself the freedom . . .

- to grow through and from relationships
- to learn from yourself as well as others
- to learn through the presence and absence of others.

Let relationships serve as mirrors for you, as teachers. And know that you are a teacher to others — not only by what you say, but by how you say things, what you don't say and how you behave.

PART III

Places And Things

If you've read this far, you've spent a fair amount of time learning how to feel good within yourself. You've also examined and practiced how to carry those lessons over into your relationships, or at least learned how to work at and be aware of those dimensions in yourself. In this section, we will begin to explore how you relate to places and things, dealing with the problem of how to maintain positive self-esteem while living in a materialistically cluttered world.

Our concern in this section is with the relationships we maintain with places and things, not with the process of acquisition — although you might find it beneficial to consider the questions of accumulation and acquisition in the context of self-worth. For example, how much do I deserve? How much do I allow myself to have? And to what extent do I identify my sense of self with the possessions I've acquired?

So what does it mean to have relationships with places and things? As with all other relationships, there is an exchange of messages. We make statements all the time — to ourselves, to others, to the places and things with which we continue to interact. How do we treat our environment? The things we use and own? The places we go? What does this say about our self-worth? What statements are we making about our own self-esteem, our place in the world, our respect for life itself?

If I feel really good about myself, I have no reason to disrespect my environment. If I feel good, there's no room to be angrily tossing possessions about. We find windows to our self-esteem in how we respond to places and things. And we can expand our sense of self and esteem as we grow in recognition and respect for the richness our environment holds and renders.

Some of the places and things to consider here include:
- your job or career
- your possessions
- the media
- your own dwelling and the houses of others, clothes, money, the environment and labels

Paying Attention

Possessions can cause us to pay attention, to notice when we're doing one thing at a time, or when we're fragmenting ourselves. When I'm doing three or more things at once, I may be good at thinking on my feet, but may be too caught up in momentum to take time to smell the flowers.

Take time to notice yourself when you are doing something with your possessions. Take time to slow yourself down, to feel your physical being, to notice with your senses. It can become almost like a meditation to become fully aware of the moment . . . brushing your teeth, making a salad, planting a garden, doing the dishes.

Do things differently. Use a different hand than your dominant one. Do things in the opposite order, so that whatever is last comes first or in the middle: Change the order of how you get dressed, how you eat your food, the errands you run.

When you change your routine, you change your point of view. Isn't that what self-esteem is about, point of view?

As you relate positively with your environment, you become more alive to your relationship with yourself, with others, with spirit. And all this adds to your sense of wholeness, to your self-esteem.

"Come To Your Senses"

We say "come to your senses!" when we want people to wake up and, as the expression goes, "Be real!" What does that phrase mean in terms of claiming the fullness of our lives?

Being blind makes me a catch-all dump for some boring and wild assumptions. Sighted people assume that my other senses are "better" than everyone else's. But we all use what we need to use. We learn to pay attention to what will help us survive. We all do this, not just those who are blind. That is part of surviving, coping and making meaning.

It has been said that we use perhaps only 10 percent of our potential. We can all use more of our senses if we choose to do so.

I've known many sighted people who get into the field of working with blind people, and soon they begin to notice with their ears many of the things that the blind people notice: the sounds of traffic, the sounds and tones of voices, the distinct hum of an air-conditioner. These aren't unique gifts of hearing, they are simply about using more of what we have.

It is also not true that people who are blind are better listeners. Some are auditory, some are not. Not all people who can see have a learning style that is based on visual acuity. The way we use our senses depends on our needs, our perceptions, our developed or undeveloped skills.

Using our senses can be a wonderful way to work out of the destructive side of self-centeredness. It's about taking time to smell the flowers. What have you taken time to notice lately?

- smells
- sights
- sounds
- tastes
- touch.

An article in the May 1990 issue of *UNITY* magazine was written by a woman who wanted to do something different for Mother's Day. Rather than prepare the usual dinner, she decided to involve all of her family's senses in that day's activities.

They were aware of the smell of each other's hair, perfume, the taste of ice cream, the sounds of their laughter and the sights of nature. The more they noticed, the deeper their love and acceptance of one another became.

Sensory Awareness

What do you notice with your senses? As you pay attention with your senses in ways that stretch your consciousness, it is impossible to feel that one day is a carbon copy of the next.

Synesthesia

Synesthesia: crossing the experience of one sense over into another. You don't have to be on drugs to appreciate this kind of thing, but you do need an imagination. Imagine that what you hear has texture. What you see has sound. What you smell has taste. This exercise can help your senses become more finely tuned.

Senses In Environment

As you listen to and notice your experiences with your senses, you may want to experiment with your atmosphere. What kind of music do you like when you're happy?

_____

_____

What kind do you like when you are feeling contemplative?

_____

_____

What kind of music do you like when you want to play or let your hair down?

_____

_____

What music do you like to hear?

_____

_____

Do you like it loud, or with the volume turned way down low?

_____

What happens if you experiment with this and try the opposite? Take a piece of your favorite music for relaxation and try turning the volume up loud. What does that feel like for you?
Do you like it? Is it relaxing?

_____

Now take a piece of music that you normally enjoy loud and play it softly. What is that like?

_____

_____

Now put on some up-beat music and lie down to take a nap. Were you able to rest? Why not? Put on some relaxation music before you attempt to do the housework or some other activity that calls for your energy. What happens?

_____

_____

_____

Some people keep the music volume up so loud they can't think or feel. They don't have to feel their aloneness. Some keep the music so jumpy, they stay in a state of adrenaline energy that resembles anger and agitation. Some people keep their music so soft and soothing, they never wake up to the rumblings they carry within.

What are your musical patterns? Do they change throughout the day? Do you like a high energy sound at times, and a more mellow sound at others?

_____

_____

_____

Listen to your mood, your needs and your preferences when choosing your music. Your self-esteem deserves more than mere background noise. Your musical selections deserve your presence, or at least your active choice.

Do you like to sing? _____

Do you sing in your shower or in your car? Are you embarrassed when you sing, or do you feel comfortable when singing?

_____

What happened in grade school when you would sing out? How about high school or church choir? Do you remember? What happened at home? Did people tease you if you were off-key? Did they tease you if you sang well, with expression? Then did you begin to hide your voice?

_____

_____

Singing comes from a real, honest place in ourselves. We cannot rehearse or analyze while we sing. We are exposed or free when we sing, depending upon our own perception. Singing can be a healing, rejuvenating way to reach in and beyond ourselves. It can be a way to connect with our Higher Self, with others, with Spirit. It can be a release, a recharge. It can be calming, relaxing. Singing can add to friendships, and be a basis for social activities.

Some people sing in the shower, in the car or all alone at home. Some people sing all the time, with musical speech. Some sing songs, or parts of songs.

It dawned on me one night at the opera that it would be interesting if people would sing their feelings to one another. I imagined a family therapy session where people would sing the things they were having a hard time saying.

Imagine voices soaring in operatic style, singing:

"Don't be so stupid!"
"I really missed you!"
"Do you love me?"
"Promise me you won't abandon me!"

With music what seems threatening can become fun.

And there's also a lot to be said for silence. Knowing when you want sound and when you want silence are important times. It's like knowing when you want people and when you want to be alone.

When do you need silence? Can you remember the last time you needed it?

_____

_____

What did you do about it?

_____

_____

How much silence do you need?
I need _____ a day.
I need _____ a week.
I don't need it.
I don't know.

Texture and color add to atmosphere. Perhaps you've noticed in restaurants, hospitals and houses, how the furnishings, colors and textures all add to the atmospheric tone.

Learn to notice the tone beyond the mere observable events by letting it speak to you emotionally and intuitively.

What kind of mood do you sense when you're suddenly in a different atmosphere? This intuition of yours is a way that your self expands, moving beyond your body and daily life, expanding your sense of self in a way that can add much to your self-definition and esteem.

What can you change in your environment that will give you a different feeling of identity? Can you change the colors in your house? Can you experiment with your clothing or makeup and see what you discover?

_____

_____

_____

As you experiment, notice not only what you like, but how your mood is affected. How does the atmosphere you create affect your conversations with others? You may want to have your colors done and find out what season you are.

The way we treat our things, the way in which we furnish our homes, the environments we frequent may serve as valuable mirrors to our self-esteem. Just as our relationships with people serve as mirrors to our own self-esteem, so it is with our environment.

Where I Live

Think of it: You live within your own skin. You live within the relationships you frequent. Let's take some time and focus on how you feel about your dwelling.

For some reason, I've always referred to where I live as "a house," even if it's only been an apartment. The word "house" just sounds homey.

How about you? What do you call the place where you live? How do you refer to it in conversation?

_____

_____

Do you feel you belong there? Is it yours? Is it someone else's? Can you call some part of it your own?

_____

_____

How do you feel about where you live?

_____

_____

Do you like where you live? What do you like?

_____

_____

What would you change?

_____

_____

Let's go on a tour.

How do you feel at the entrance way? Is it a welcoming entrance? Can you remember when you first walked into that room for the very first time? How did you feel about yourself at that time? Did you think your life would be pleasant as you lived in that place? What do you see as you walk in?

_____

What do you feel under your feet?

What do you smell? Is there a smell that brings memories to mind?

Now walk through your living room. Is it a room that has been allowed for living? What kinds of memories do you have as you stand in this room? What is the furniture like? Is it comfortable and inviting? Is it hard and cold? What do you see? What do you feel? What is on the walls? Does music play in this room? If so, what kind?

Now move to the doorway of your kitchen. What can you remember as you stand in this spot? Have you been nourished by this kitchen? Has there been joy and hospitality here? What about community? Have you learned in this kitchen — to love your body more, to treat it wisely, respecting what it needs in the way of food and what it does not?

And what about the dining room or the table where you eat? Can you remember times when you've sat alone at this table? What is the view? What memories do you have of tastes? What conversations have gone on here? Are there some that are particularly meaningful?

Now move through the doorway and into your bedroom. Is this a safe room? Is it one where you've been able to feel loved, safe, free? Is it a room where you've been able to be playful? What do you see? What is the room like? What do you smell? How is it furnished? Does it invite good feelings? Does it proudly display your self-esteem? What would make it even more comfortable for you? Are there secrets that have been held in this room? Are they secrets that are okay for you to live with? Do they weigh you down? Are there secrets that would be better off out in the open somewhere? Are there closets in this room? What's in them?

Are there symbolic closets in this room? Are there closets in this room that you've come out of, or closets that you know you can move in and out of as you choose? Remember that honesty is about self-honesty first, then honesty with others as it is best for you.

_____

_____

_____

Now move to the doorway of your bathroom. Here is a room that has been here for you to get rid of what you don't need and offered a space for you to take care of your body. What feelings do you have about this room? Have you felt safe in here? Has it been a private place? What memories do you have of this room? Are there special moments when you've nurtured yourself or received nurturance from someone? What kinds of things do you see as you walk in here? Do you have decorations? What about your belongings? How do you display them or put them away? Do you have a favorite fragrance? There are lots of smells in bathrooms. Do you know you don't have to hide your own body odors? Do you like the door closed when you're in there? Do you like it left open? How about when you're not in there? Do you like the door closed when you're not in there? Why?

_____

_____

_____

Now move through some of the other rooms in your house. What is special about them? What memories come to mind about these rooms? Who occupies these rooms? Do they belong to you? Do they add to your self-esteem? Are there treasures of yours in them? Have you enjoyed special moments in them? What possessions are comforting or enjoyable to you in these rooms?

_____

_____

_____

What have you collected?
- figurines
- stuffed animals
- dolls
- coins
- stamps

- paintings
- carvings
- Other:

_____

_____

Has the nature of what you've collected changed over time? Do you collect different things today than you did five years ago? How about ten years ago? And if you still collect the same articles, has your taste changed in terms of characteristics?

What similarities and differences are there about the things you've collected?

_____

_____

_____

How do you feel about your belongings? How are they positioned throughout your space?

- cluttered
- proudly displayed
- neatly put away
- tossed into closets, drawers and under beds
- easily lost

_____

_____

_____

How do you treat your possessions when you're angry?

I cling to them.
I hide behind them.
I slam them around.
I break them.
I clean house.
I haven't noticed.
Other:

_____

_____

Are you more careful with some possessions than others? What are they? Why are you more careful?

_____

_____

_____

How about lending possessions? Do you easily lend? Are you careful about who you lend to, and what you will and will not lend?

What are some things you will not lend?

_____

_____

Why not?

And how about borrowing from others? How do you feel about borrowing? Do you ask easily? Do you return what you borrow? How do you care for the things you borrow?

Where do you keep your car, if you have one? Does it have a place all its own? Is it protected? What is your car like? How do you feel about it? Does it add to your self-esteem in some way? What do you have in your car? Many people like to carry all sorts of stuff with them. When was the last time you went through your car and discarded what you don't need? What is in your car that you enjoy? Is your car a place where you can be you? Do you usually drive it? Are you often alone in it?

_____

_____

_____

How about when you go to the dwellings of others? What is that like for you?

Do you enjoy looking around? Can you think of houses where you've gone and enjoyed particular experiences with your senses?

Whose house do you love to look at? Who has the view you love?

Who has the carpet you love to feel with your feet? And whose house do you love to go to for good meals? Whose house gives you a feeling that it's okay to feel at home? Whose house do you feel loved and affirmed in?

_____

_____

_____

_____

_____

_____

How do you treat these dwellings? Are you kinder to other people's possessions than you are to your own? Do you respect the furnishings and belongings of others?

_____

_____

_____

How do you feel about your own house as you consider the dwellings of other people? Are you envious? Are you proud of your own?

_____

_____

_____

_____

_____

_____

There is one perspective that says people are distracted by having too many things, by a preoccupation with their environment. But be careful what you ask for here. There are ways to learn balance with our material possessions without getting rid of them through a crisis. Saying that you want to "get rid of" your clutter could bring disaster into your life that rids you of possessions without your ever having the right to choose and weed out what is no longer needed or wanted.

What about food? Have you ever considered that you have a relationship with food? It is one of the things in your environment that mirrors your self-esteem.

Do you enjoy eating? What are your eating patterns? How many times a day do you usually eat?

_____ I eat regular meals.

_____ I snack and nibble.

_____ I don't eat regularly.

_____ I forget to eat.

_____ I live to eat.

What are some of your favorite foods?

_____

_____

What memories come to mind as you think of these foods? Do you have special emotional memories of those foods from childhood? Did someone important feed you those foods? Did you have fun with certain foods where you still carry the memory?

Can you think of some foods that you don't like? What memories do you associate with those foods?

What, Changing Tastes?

What about your own tastes? Have you noticed changes in what you like and don't like?

Can you think of things you've outgrown? How about things you've moved away from?

Some things don't taste the same as they did when we were little. How about things like:

> fried onions out of the can
> brown sugar out of the box
> sugar cubes
> candy corn on Halloween

Or how about paste that came in those big jars in grade school? Play dough?

Do you still like those things? All of them? Any of them?

And perhaps there are foods you used to turn your nose up at that now you like:

> _____ spinach
> _____ carrots
> _____ liver
> _____ tofu
> _____ decaffeinated drinks
> _____ water
> _____ food or drinks without sugar
> _____ other

_____

_____

Have you ever noticed your emotions changing with the food you eat?

_____

What have you noticed? How do your emotions change, and with what foods?

_____

_____

How do you eat? Do you gobble? Do you eat slowly? Do you eat all the food on your plate? Do you pick at your food?

In a presentation called "Junk-food Communication: Deep-Fried Feelings and Interpersonal Indigestion," I maintain that there is a relationship between how and what we eat and our emotional nature and relationship patterns. For instance, people who eat fast all the time probably struggle with perfectionism, with fear of loss if they don't get in there immediately. Picky eaters may be sitting on the emotional edges of life, having a hard time getting more directly involved with the experience of tasting and living.

And what about all those things we swallow that are not good for us, and the stuff we continue to "dish out" to others? Our food choices may well be windows to patterns we follow. Do you swallow putdowns and verbal abuse? Do you dish out critical remarks and gossip? Do you go for the fast-food convenient intimacy that leaves you with a bad aftertaste? Do you settle for crumbs, for crummy or crumbly relationships? Do you know you are worthy of much more than crumbs? How about an abundant feast?

Let's take another look at body image. What is the purpose of your body? Why carry it around day in and day out? And if there is a purpose for having a body, then why not consider the food and its effects on our bodies?

_____

_____

_____

_____

Let's move on from food and look at other aspects of our lives. Are there any rules, beliefs or patterns that you once rejected, but which now seem pretty good to you?

There is the Mark Twain joke about suddenly seeing parents after several years and remarking, "It's amazing how much they learned! How much they grew!"

We do the growing. Hopefully, they do so too. But whether they do or not, we can!

Money

Think of the paper and coins that pass through our hands from day to day. Think of all the people who touch the same money we touch, and all the money that comes into and goes out from our lives. With such a flow of this powerful substance, we need to know how we feel about it. Whether for business or consumers, money is a powerful presence in our lives.

How do you feel about money? Can you fathom the thought that your relationship to it mirrors your self-esteem? It's one concrete measure to show how worthy you believe yourself to be. Are you meant to have money? Do you believe you deserve it? Or is money only for those who are "lucky"?

What happens when you think of winning the lottery? Do you just laugh at the thought, as though you are being too grandiose to plan on it?

Money Messages

Take time to consider what it was like to learn about money as a child. Was money available in your childhood? What messages did you get about money?

_____

_____

_____

How was money available? Was it worked for? Were you in touch with how money got into your household?

_____

_____

_____

Did you get an allowance? Who gave it to you? How much was it? Can you remember what you did with it? Did it matter to anyone what you did with it? Did you plan, set goals about how you would handle or save it?

Did you have to do something to "get" this allowance? Some kids have to do chores to "earn" it and for others it is a "given." How about you?

_____

_____

_____

_____

How old were you when you began working outside of the home to generate money?

_____

What was that work like? Why did you start to work? Did you want to work? Did your family need you to work? Could you keep the money from when you worked for your own needs and wants?

Were you free to choose what you did with your money?

_____

_____

_____

Was there enough to eat?

_____

_____

What kinds of clothes did you wear?

_____

_____

How did you feel with your peers when it came to money? Did it matter what you wore? Were you accepted for who you were?

_____

_____

_____

I felt I had to have a certain "look" to be accepted.
I always wore hand-me-downs.
I felt I passed. I made the mark.
I tried to "look" like we had money.
I felt ashamed of being "poor."

What did people tell you about money?
Money is evil.
Money is power.
Money is only for the "lucky."
Money depends upon who you know.
Money is unlimited.
Money is scarce.

Now complete the following statement:

Money is _____.

What did you decide about other people based on their money or lack
of it?

"They have money, they must be happy."
"They are just miserable. They have all that money and are so unhappy."
"They don't have money, therefore they're uneducated, stupid, not
worthy . . ."
"They have money. They've made it!"

Chances are that whatever you heard is still with you in some measure.
What would you do with a lot of money? _____

_____

_____

How much do you need? _____

_____

_____

How much do you want? _____

_____

_____

What do you already do with your money? _____

_____

_____

_____

Do you bury your head and let it come and go?
Do you watch it to the point where it disallows you any spontaneity?
Do you buy other people presents?
How about presents for you? Are they okay to buy?

_____

_____

_____

_____

The key here is balance. And as you strive to gain or maintain balance, it
doesn't mean you can't have abundance. On the contrary, building self-

esteem means comprehending that you have the right to abundance. It means respecting your best self, other people, and the environment. If I grab for possessions in a greedy way, I am not respecting myself, my environment nor the true value of money. Grabbing without respect cannot be a mirror for positive self-esteem.

What will it take to bring more balance into your life with money? It may take different things on different days.

If you buy presents for other people most of the time, why not buy a gift for yourself instead? If you buy easily for yourself, why not put that pattern aside and buy something for someone else?

What was the last thing you bought yourself? How much did it cost?

_____

_____

_____

And what did you buy for yourself before that?

_____

_____

_____

What was the last gift you bought someone else?

_____

_____

_____

How do you feel when you buy for yourself?
    I feel guilty.
    I feel great!
    I am excited.
    I feel unworthy.

_____

_____

How do you feel when you buy something for someone else?
    I feel good.
    It gives me joy.
    I wish it was me getting the gift.
    I worry about finances.
    I resent them for "receiving."
    I can't wait to see their joy in receiving.

_____

_____

When was the last time you felt you spent too much money?

_____

_____

What was the situation? _____

_____

_____

How much did you spend? _____

Looking back, were you shaming yourself, or did you really spend more than you feel is best for you to spend?

_____

_____

Saying No To Money

Again, as in all relationships, we need to be able to say no to requests for our money when it is not in our best interest to say yes.

What happens to your self esteem when someone asks you for money? Do you feel guilty when someone with a "good cause" tells you to "search your heart"? You needn't be governed by pressure.

This also means that sometimes we say no to our own requests for spending. How do you feel when you know that by saying no to yourself, you're missing out on a pleasure or a product that you have wanted?

Is it inconvenient?_____

_____

Do you feel a sense of loss?_____

_____

Do you feel a sense of deprivation?_____

_____

What role models did you have for wise use of money? Did anyone in your house demonstrate to you that they could live with delayed gratification?

Simple Pleasures

There is a real challenge and delight in finding simple pleasures that don't cost money. Can you remember as a child having all sorts of fun with a plain old cardboard box? What do you like to do today that costs little or no money?

I like to go for a walk.

I like to sing.

I like to reread books I've loved over the years.

I like to write.

I like to talk with people I feel close to.

Other:

_____

_____

_____

Magnetism Of Gratitude

There is something about appreciating what we have that allows it to multiply. Think of abundance as something that carries over far beyond mere financial resources. See it as something that includes all the ways you enjoy possessions, ideas, talents, intuition and sensory awareness. As you know you are rich in other areas of your life, you are able to draw to you any number of possibilities.

Choices About Seduction

If you buy the notion that we are always in relationships with ourselves, each other and our environment, then perhaps you have considered how there are numerous attempts by all of these influences to seduce you, to persuade you.

Seduction is wonderful. It can give you "magical" feelings, let you take a vacation from the "work" side of your life. And it is especially wonderful when chosen by you.

As we discussed when talking about sexuality, the bulk of what's important is what's between our ears. And so it is with seduction continuing beyond the bedroom with other aspects of our environment.

The Media

Once when working in radio, the producer said to me: "We decide what we want the audience to believe and then we say it to them over and over so they will."

This is quite different from "We repeatedly affirm what is true."

Being seduced is being "brought" into what someone else would have us to believe.

As we give up our power and move into what someone else would have us believe, we are letting others affect our self-esteem.

The media gives us messages about what is okay, who the winners are, who the beautiful people are. We get messages about what is "in," what all the successful people are buying, doing, feeling, thinking . . .

And we get other more subtle messages.

The cable TV shopping channels appeal to our desire for nurturance, for family, for relatedness. Available 24 hours a day, they are there to encourage us to have those things that will feel good to us, look good on us, make our lives easier. If you listen to the callers, you will notice how many of them have become seduced into believing that they have a relationship with the hosts, that they are saving money as they continue to buy increasing numbers of products, and that they are comforted when that host is there for them when they cannot sleep. How clever these channels are at giving the illusion that there is a sense of community.

So do we give up these channels, or anything else that is attempting to seduce us? Absolutely not! We learn to enjoy them. We learn to make choices to allow us to buy and to say no.

We may indeed decide to have a rapport with on-air personalities. But there is a difference between fantasy and day-to-day rapport-building. There is a difference between people who know us giving us feedback on what looks good on us, what might be helpful to us in our lives, and our letting the pressure of the media dictate our needs and well-being.

How Do You Feel About Clothes?

Do you know that you are more than what you wear? Do you feel that if you don't wear the right thing you aren't worth noticing? Do you believe that if you wear the right thing then maybe someone, whoever it is, will find you lovable, acceptable, okay? Do you have to wear something new all the time so people won't think you don't have enough clothes? So that maybe someone will be impressed? What do you wear if you're going to not be concerned about what other people think? What do you wear when you want to relax?

Again, we can return to our discussion about body image. Often how we feel about ourselves with or without clothes can tie in with our body image. How do you feel about your body when you have no clothes on at all? Is anyone allowed to see you, to be with you? Do you need the lights to be off?

Do you also respect your boundaries and those of others about your body? Good self-esteem depends upon a balance between openness and discretion.

How do you feel about make-up, perfume, jewelry and other accessories? How much are they a part of your life? In what way do they add to your life? What would it be like to be without them?

_____

_____

_____

_____

Knowing how we dress and feel about ourselves in various situations is part of sorting the various ways we live, both in our private and professional lives. While healthy self-esteem depends largely on how we feel about ourselves, it also means that we know we are not isolated, living alone on individual islands. This means that we take responsibility for what we choose to project in our appearance, behavior and attitudes.

We've talked a lot about many of these things within the realm of our lives, but what about going to work every day? How do you feel about that? What is "work" about for you in your life?

My Uniform

It came to me one day that "blindness is my uniform," something I agreed to wear in this life to do the work I'm here to do. This isn't about martyrdom. It's about knowing what my job is, what my role is, my uniform to do my work, and most especially, that I am more than my uniform, more than my job.

For me this means that I believe I'm here to see and help others to see in new ways. My work on a daily basis always ties in with "seeing." Whether I am counseling, speaking, writing, or just talking with a friend, I know that my uniform is with me, and that it is not the bottom line to who or what I am.

Your Job?

What does it mean to "go to work"? We often refer to "work" as the opposite to "play." So do we assume then, that "work" is not fun?

Sigmund Freud said that we need a balance between love and work. What do you think he meant by this in terms of our mental/emotional health?

Once I had a job that I hated. People would say to me, "Well, most people don't like their jobs." If that's true, and if we're in "not fun" situations much of the time, then how do we cultivate or maintain self-esteem at this thing we call "work"?

For some people, "work" means day-to-day drudgery. For some, it is purely a means to get income. Work to some is the way they experience self-esteem. For some, work is a sense of community, a place for social bonding. And for others, work is quite separate from personal life.

What is "work" for you?

_____

_____

_____

_____

_____

Some people differentiate between a job, a career, a vocation or an occupation. What do each of these terms mean to you?

_____

_____

_____

_____

_____

How do you think of hobbies? Is a hobby something you do only for fun? I often hear hobbies talked about as though they're relegated to a "less-than-the-best" status. If you do it for fun, is that somehow less important than doing it for "work"? And what if you happen to love your work? Is that different than a hobby? If something in your life is a hobby, is it okay to make money from it?

What are hobbies in your life?

_____

_____

Do you get paid for them?

_____

Are some of your hobbies a part of your work?

_____

_____

_____

Is that answer okay?

_____

_____

_____

And what do you do for leisure?

_____

_____

_____

How often? _____

_____

_____

A commercial for a health spa once had a little jingle that said, "We put a little play in your day." How do you play? Is play the same as leisure for you?

_____

_____

_____

_____

For me, play is broader than leisure. I play with words, with ideas, with mental pictures, with voices . . . I play through much of my work. How about you? How do you play?

_____

_____

_____

_____

Playfulness makes it possible to feel good, to maintain and build self-esteem through a wide array of life's activities and demands. Play makes it possible to love work, to act with a deep sense of joy.

Some people prefer to love what they do most of the time. Some people feel fine about doing work that is separate from joy. For the good of your self-esteem, it's important for you to know what you need.

Do you emotionally need to work? _____

Is work important to your intellectual needs? _____

_____

Is work important to you socially? How much do you need to be working around or with other people?

_____

_____

_____

Is work important to you spiritually? Does it matter that you work in terms of life purpose or beliefs?

_____

_____

_____

How about fun with work? Is that okay? Do you have fun at work? Can you have more fun at work and still do your job well?

_____

_____

_____

What goals do you have about work? What lifelong ambitions?

_____

_____

_____

Where do you want to be with your life as you grow older? Do you expect you'll retire? At what age? What do you envision life to be like as you grow older? What goals do you have? What mental pictures or dreams?

_____

_____

_____

What do you feel "work" expects from you?
    perfection
    twenty-four-hours-a-day commitment
    total dedication
    loyalty
    happy face and cheerful attitude
    early or prompt meeting of deadlines

to take care of the boss
to always behave "appropriately"
Other:

_____

_____

Was there enough room here to write the list of expectations you carry? Are the expectations you carry about work realistic?

_____

_____

_____

Where did these expectations come from? Who said that you "should do or be," or "should accomplish"?

_____

_____

_____

On the other hand, have you ever felt that it doesn't matter what you do at work?

_____

_____

_____

What happens to your self-esteem?

_____

_____

_____

What do you need to do so that work in your life can add, or at least, does not eat at your self-esteem?
- Work in a place where the goals are in harmony with my beliefs.
- Set boundaries on my emotional commitment, my time and energy.
- Communicate more regularly and honestly about the problems I'm having at work.
- Stretch my accomplishments by adding some goals and projects that will stimulate my intelligence.
- Have more fun at work.
- Have more fun away from work.
- Take better care of my health.

- Work more comfortably for a woman.
- Work more comfortably for a man.
- Work best as a leader.
- Work best as a follower.

_____

_____

What skills do you have that add to your self-esteem at work when you're allowed to access and show them?

_____

_____

_____

What skills do you have that show you're especially good at leading or at following?

_____

_____

_____

_____

_____

Do you know it's okay to let people know what your skills are?
    Yes.
    No.
    I'm not supposed to blow my own horn.

Is your life more than a day-to-day job? Perhaps a day-to-day job is exactly what you want, without the stress or worry of a job that expects more from you.

_____

_____

Whichever the case may be, you are "more than" any roles you play or any uniform you wear.

It became important for me to learn when working a day-to-day job that I work "for myself" and work "at my place of employment." This means that I can responsibly wear my uniform, do my job, and know that it does not comprise my whole identity. Another way of saying this is to consider roles. A role is something you take on, but it is not who you are. You take on a role at work to do a job.

At work, while you take on your role, you have a right to your own self-esteem. Playing a role does not mean that you put "you" or your self-esteem on the shelf. It means that you accept your responsibilities as they make sense to you, but you are still connected with your self-esteem. Your self still deserves your attention and respect while you do your job and "play" your role at "work."

In a day-to-day sense, what is your job? What kinds of jobs have you had in the past?

_____

_____

_____

How have you felt about yourself when you've had these jobs? How do you feel about yourself now in your present or most recent job?

_____

_____

_____

If you're not working now, how do you feel about yourself? How have you felt at times if you weren't working? If you are self-employed, what's it like for you when people say, "Oh, you're not working," because your schedule is different? If you are retired, what's it like for you to leave a job or career, to put aside a major way you've been known by others, a large part of how you've spent your time? Has your personal or social life changed?

_____

_____

_____

_____

Do you have a career? Is your work more than just a job?

_____

_____

How do you feel when you're not at work? Is it okay to be more than your career?

_____

_____

Do you ever get tired of your role? Do you ever need to know that people know you beyond your role?

_____

Labels

Roles are a form of labels. Suppose a minister walks into a room where people are laughing. Suddenly, the room gets quiet. It is assumed that because the "minister" walks in, there is no place for humor or light conversation. This means that the "minister" is a label perceived and not a person who is playing a role, wearing a uniform.

What about labels in your life? You are a son, a daughter . . . what is that like for you? Have you ever needed to know you were more than a son or a daughter?

_____

_____

_____

Perhaps you are a parent. I've known parents say to their kids, "Okay, for today, or until I say when, I'm going to be a person and not just a parent. Call me by my first name."

Are you a brother or a sister? Are you a man or a woman? A boy or a girl? Do you wish people would know that you are more than those labels?

And how about the age you are now? Does that carry expectations that put you in a box with a label?

_____

_____

_____

_____

And how about other labels in your life?
- sexual orientation: gay/lesbian, bisexual, straight
- racial, ethnic or cultural background

_____

_____

labels of recovery: alcoholic, addict, ACoA, co-dependent . . .

_____

labels of living with disability (physical, emotional, developmental or others) that go unrecognized

_____

labels of religious life

_____

labels of illness

_____

labels of fame

_____

labels of association: does the label of the person you live with label you?

_____

When have you felt labeled? Call to mind a situation. Did you feel reduced? Misunderstood? Were assumptions made about your capability or limitations?

_____

_____

_____

_____

Were decisions made for or about you?

_____

_____

How did you feel about being labeled?

_____

_____

_____

How did you handle your feelings about being labeled?

_____

_____

_____

What would you like to say if this happens again?

_____

_____

_____

Are there ways you can take care of yourself differently to minimize the chances of being labeled?

_____

_____

_____

What would you like others to know about you?
    I'm a person.
    I am not defined by a label, a statistic or a mold.
    I have moods and feelings, needs and desires.
    I have abilities and limitations.
    I am a sexual person.
    I am changeable.
    Other:

_____

_____

_____

_____

Granted, we live in a world of people and circumstances where we cannot guarantee that we will not be mislabeled or even reduced by others. Yet as we build a rich foundation of self-esteem, we learn to make choices about people, places and things that will foster our self-esteem and allow it to flourish.

Your uniform has something to say about the work you do, the career you have and the role you play. But be it a career, a role or a life circumstance that serves as a catalyst for labeling, you are more than your uniform or your label. Uniforms and labels can help with functional organization, but there is no mandate that they be used in dysfunctional ways. Good healthy self-esteem depends upon each of us knowing that we are more than our uniforms, roles and labels.

Growing In Self-Esteem

As we grow in self-esteem, we find that we are affected by the ways in which we relate with places and things, as well as how we relate with people and with ourselves. Often we project our attitudes on the places where we live, work and visit, and on the things we do and use. Our possessions, our money, our clothes and our accessories all give us information into our patterns and beliefs that may be continuing to affect our self-esteem. In turn, we realize that our behavior patterns with places and things have their consequences or outcomes, and that to grow rich in self-esteem, we can become more response-able so that the consequences we experience affect our self-esteem in ways that are positive and fulfilling.

PART IV

The School Of Life

"What's It All About, Alfie?"

Remember that old song? How many times have you asked yourself what it's all about? Why do we learn all these lessons? What purpose is there for any of us?

There is no "right" answer. What is one person's disbelief is another's belief. You may never know what is actual, what is "real." But knowing what you believe, what makes sense to you is an important part of self-esteem.

I don't believe that one single facet of creation was intended to be wasted. Orgasm shows us that sex is meant to be joyful. Pain shows us that we need to reach toward healing. Disabilities of all types show us that being able is beyond our assumed senses or human faculties.

A puzzle piece that doesn't seem to fit is an invitation to stretch in vision and faith. How do you make sense out of all the pieces of your life, so that you can go forward and believe that your life has some sense, continuity, meaning and purpose?

It's not important to regurgitate what anyone else has told you about "the way it is," or what you've read in any book. If you've chosen to accept what someone has said to you or what you've been told, then that's one way of making it truly yours. This book is a place to sort out your beliefs and discover what the school of life is all about for you.

Words And Beliefs

Think about these words and what they mean to you:

God
Spirit
spirit
prayer
church
Christmas
Easter
heaven
hell
purgatory
sin
peace
beliefs
reincarnation
destiny
karma
psychic
death
intuition
religion
rituals
Bible
devil
Satan
confession
communion
tribulation
Passover
Second Coming
commandments
Christian
Jewish
organized religion
interdenominational
agnostic

atheistic
nondenominational
Spiritualist
being "saved"
salvation
"the Word of God"
grace
baptism
confirmation
evolution
amen
sacrament
cross
minister
preacher
priest
nun
revelations
"spread the word"
Lord
lord
reverence
congregation
pledge
witness
offering
recovery
Higher Power
Source
white light
eternal life
Other:

_____

_____

_____

_____

_____

_____

What assumptions do you have about these words? Perhaps some of them take you back to memories of what you learned.

What did you learn about these words when you were growing up? What did you hear, if anything, about what you were supposed to believe?

_____

_____

_____

_____

What did you see? Did the adults do the same things they instructed you to do?

_____

_____

_____

_____

_____

_____

Religious Messages

What messages were you given about church or synagogue?

_____

_____

Did you go to church or synagogue as a child?
Did you go regularly? If so, how often?
    weekly
    monthly
    only on special occasions

_____

What do you remember about going to church or synagogue?
What was your experience in terms of your feelings, impressions and perceptions?

_____

_____

_____

   How did you feel about the people there? Do any vivid memories, positive or negative, come to mind?

_____

_____

   How did you feel about the messages or beliefs of the church or synagogue?

_____

_____

   What, if any, components made sense to you?

_____

_____

   What was hard to understand?

_____

_____

   What didn't you agree with?

_____

_____

   What is still confusing today?

_____

_____

   Are there things you still really do not agree with that you've been expected to believe?

_____

_____

_____

What are you expected to believe today?

_____

_____

How are you supposed to demonstrate your beliefs?

_____

_____

What was your favorite part of what you heard or what you learned?

_____

_____

Is that still with you today?

_____

_____

What reflections about any of this would you like to add here?

_____

_____

What did you grow up learning about God? What did you hear about God?

_____

_____

Where did you hear it?

_____

_____

_____

If you didn't hear about God much in your home, how did you feel when your friends would talk about the God they talked to or the "church" things they did?

    I envied them.

    I was relieved it wasn't me.

    I thought it sounded stupid.

    I secretly had my own beliefs.

_____

_____

_____

_____

Where did you hear about God?

_____

_____

    At home?

    In church or synagogue?

    In school?

_____

_____

    Other:

_____

_____

Who told you about God?

_____

_____

_____

What kinds of different things did people say?

_____

_____

_____

"God is good."
"God is angry!"
"God is love."
"God is an 'it'."
"God is a 'he'."
"God is a 'she'."
"God punishes us."
"God judges us."

What did you experience or imagine in terms of God's presence?

Did you imagine a voice? _____

Did you imagine a beam of light? _____

What did you picture? _____

Did you imagine an old man sitting on a throne? _____

_____

What other ways did you imagine or experience a presence? _____

_____

Where did God live or hang out? _____

_____

Can you imagine how you would've answered these questions as a child if anyone asked you what you thought God did all day?

_____

_____

_____

What did you feel about God?

_____

_____

_____

Were you ever mad at God?

_____

_____

What was that like?

_____

How did you imagine God felt about you?

How did you imagine God felt if you were mad at God?

Was it important?

If you didn't believe in God, then how did you feel about all of the people and the messages others gave you about believing?

I envied them.

I thought they were insecure.

I thought they were stupid.

I thought someone had brainwashed them.

I considered myself "lucky."

Other:

What did you believe would happen to you when you died?
    Nothing.
    I'd go to heaven.
    I'd go to hell.
    I'd go to purgatory.
    I'd come back here again.
    I don't know.
    I don't care.
    Other:

_____

_____

_____

What did you believe you would deserve?
    The peace and joy of heaven.
    To burn in hell forever.
    To get what I deserve in this life only.
    I get what I deserve from life itself.
    Other:

_____

_____

_____

What did you learn about prayer when you were growing up?

_____

_____

Was it a rule in your house? Was it expected daily?

_____

_____

Were prayers memorized? Did you pray out loud or was it always someone else?

_____

Did your family pray often, or only on special occasions such as Thanksgiving?

In my house I was expected to pray on holidays or when I was in trouble. If I had done something wrong, I was supposed to pray then because I had been bad, would be punished, or should feel ashamed.

What do you remember from your experience?

Who taught you about prayer?

Was it more important to pray at any particular time of day?

How did you feel about praying out loud?

I felt proud.
I felt fake.
I felt stupid.
I felt peaceful.
I felt connected with others.
I felt connected with God.
I resented that it was always me.

_____

_____

_____

How did you feel about praying by yourself when you were alone?
    Peaceful.
    I never did it.
    Awkward.
    Okay, as long as I could read it out of a book.
    At a loss for words.
    At home.
    Grounded in a sense of self.

_____

_____

Did you feel it helped? Did it matter? Did it seem like a game, or just another set of rules?

_____

_____

What can you remember about whether or not you felt you were heard when you prayed?

_____

_____

_____

_____

If you felt you were heard, how did you know? What was your clue?

_____

_____

_____

_____

When did you feel you weren't heard?

_____

_____

_____

_____

What did you do or decide when you felt you were not heard?

_____

_____

_____

What about other rituals? Are there other things you were taught or that you did as a child concerning religion or your spiritual life?

_____

_____

_____

What was it like to grow up with other kids who did or did not have the same rituals as you?

_____

_____

_____

Did you read the Bible?

_____

_____

How did you feel about the Bible?

_____

_____

Did you go to Sunday school?

_____

Did you go to parochial school?

_____

Does anything else stand out in your memories that you wish to make note of here?

_____

_____

_____

_____

Remember that the messages you have been used to hearing have an effect on your self-esteem. If someone follows you around all day and tells you you're a jerk, you have a few choices. You can try to ignore both the message, the messenger and your own personal reaction. You can try and become more noisy than the messenger. You can be defensive, hoping that this way you won't give the message power. Or you can work with all of it so that you aren't wasting time and energy and valuable self-esteem.

If you've believed that some patriarchal figure is watching and waiting to punish you or even reward you, based on perfection or imperfection, then it is no wonder if you don't feel intimate with spirituality. Who wants to feel intimate, much less peaceful, with something or someone who is mean, cruel or unfriendly? It would be easy to understand getting stuck into still wanting approval from an unloving source. Some of us still try to get those who were abusive to love us; but an intimate, peace-filled bond, based on deep trust only develops with life on a foundation of genuine self-esteem.

Now, on that ever-growing foundation of self-esteem, it is time to clear out any subtle old ways in which you may still be operating on beliefs in a God or in a doctrine that negates you as the acceptable person you are today.

We've been looking at self-esteem based on relationships. What is your relationship, if any, with your spirituality? With the universe, God, whatever you choose to call it, or however you see it through your beliefs?

_____

_____

_____

What, if anything, do you choose to call it?

_____

_____

_____

If you have this relationship with God, or whatever you choose to call it, why not write someone a letter, and tell him/her/it how you feel about this relationship?

First write a letter as though you're that child again, with whatever feelings you had as a child that you want God to know. Remember to put in your concerns, confusion, hopes, dreams . . . whatever you feel is important. Also remember to put in your anger, or simply write and say you don't want to do anything else to acknowledge God. The point here is not to be "right" but merely to express how you feel.

_____

_____

_____

_____

_____

Now write a letter as the adult you are today. What do you want? Need? What do you think this significant other needs or wants from you? For example:

I want more clarity of messages, purpose and meaning.

I want to feel less alone, more connected.

I think God wants me to trust that the messages are coming through, to listen more quietly and intently.

I believe God wants me to know that I am an expression of God, that I am here for a purpose, that I have value and worth.

Now write your letter:

_____

_____

_____

_____

_____

God Within

Traditional religion would have us believe that God is separate from us, that we strayed from and need this external force to keep us on track. Is there not truth in that at times? Are there moments when we need structure, limits, direction and help?

The new holistic movement would say that God is within us, that our potential is already right within us to be more than we have known ourselves to be. Can you fathom that possibility as well? Can you imagine that the potential to become who you really are is already within you?

Sometimes we need to develop our emotional and spiritual muscles.

Sometimes we need to stretch beyond our conscious selves. Other times we need to relax and allow loved ones and Spirit to nourish us.

Perhaps there does not have to be such tension between the old and the new. As they say in 12-Step programs, "Take what you like and leave the rest."

The confusion about religion and spirituality can be a marvelous opportunity to grow in self-esteem and spiritual growth.

Growing in self-esteem isn't just about ego embellishment. It's about being grounded, standing on solid footing, personal integrity and broad vision. So growing in self-esteem doesn't need to conflict with spiritual growth. Growing in self-esteem does not need to imply that we become more selfish and arrogant. It actually means embracing ourselves more fully so that we can truly be receptive to the messages and works of Spirit.

Imagine that you are in a hallway surrounded by doors. They are closed right now, but not locked. It seems dark because when the doors are closed, you can't see what's on the other side of them. One door is marked, "God Within." One door is marked, "The Bible!" One door is marked, "Parental figures." There are doors for every church or synagogue that has ever influenced you.

One door is marked, "Atheism," another "Agnosticism." Now turn in circles in front of all these doors and feel the confusion. Perhaps behind one of those doors, or in the hallway behind you, there are some folks clamoring, telling you how to make up your mind, leading you to think that your self-esteem is packaged and tightly wrapped, waiting for you behind one of those doors.

But your confusion is putting your assumptions on hold. It is allowing you to sort through the muddle to find what works for you. Perhaps you will find your answers — and I believe you will find more than one — behind one or more of these doors. You can move in and out of lots of doors. This is a giant mansion, and you are not limited to one door, one room, one belief system.

How do you feel about yourself as you find yourself considering these issues? Do you feel guilty? Excited? Both?

If there were only one way to be in the world, then we would all have been made alike. But the fact that we all are made different can serve as permission that it's okay to be different and live with positive self-esteem and integrity.

Spirit

What does it mean to "spread the word"? I believe there is much broadening that can be done with this concept. Do you know that every time you smile, laugh or express something positive to someone that you are "spreading the word"? You are spreading the word of "good," spreading "goodness," spreading a "good" "spirit" of life.

If ever we think we are spreading the word by merely reciting jargon, we may as well be taking pills. What are pills but encapsulated chemicals, prepackaged, precalculated, nonfeeling, nonhuman answers to human struggle. When we resort to reciting prepackaged jargon, we are giving our creativity away and hoping that canned expression will save us from our own self-searching process.

If you believe that spreading the word is about sharing the Bible, then that is your own particular way of spreading the word. But your self-esteem will profit and blossom as the meaning of what you are saying comes from within "you," and not from whatever you happened to have memorized.

The Bible, or any other text, comes alive, becomes truly real and present so long as we are willing to find the very personal meaning it has from deep within us.

Self-esteem is not to be found in superficial recitation. Spreading the word and growing in self-esteem are not about self righteously spouting off polished platitudes or cliches.

Say It Differently

Take a phrase that means a lot to you and see how many other ways you can find to say the same thing. See how many other names you can find for what you experience as God, your Higher Power, or your higher Self. Find ways to say things that move you out of jargon and into your own self expression. If you have favorite prayers or passages, put them into other words. See how you can let your intuitive self find a deeper meaning for these words. If you can't find personal meaning, then put them aside and search for things that do have meaning.

One of the best ways I know of to find beliefs of your own has to do with noticing how you live and how you feel about life. If you don't know about Spirit, as in "Holy Spirit," then think about spirit in other ways. What kind of spirit or mood is important for you to live with and project to the world? What about "team spirit"? Do you believe in that? What about "holiday spirit"? We use the word "spirit" when we talk about moods, holidays, team effort. What if we take away the word "holy" and put in "wholeness"? What comes to mind if you think of anything in the spirit of wholeness? Does that lighten the picture? Is it clearer? We can think of what we do, how we take care of ourselves, how we grow in loving others and gain clarity by looking within ourselves for ways to act from a spirit of wholeness. When you think of a spirit of wholeness adding to your life, how do you want to do things differently?

Eating: _____

_____

_____

_____

Working: _____

_____

_____

_____

Playing: _____

_____

_____

_____

Being a friend: _____

_____

_____

_____

Growing in a sense of meaning and purpose: _____

_____

_____

_____

Loving yourself: _____

_____

_____

Some people like to think of God as being synonymous with "good."
Just add an o to God and you've got good. "Oh, good!"
God = g.o.d. = good orderly direction.
Sin: = s.i.n. = self-inflicted nonsense or self-induced negation.
    What old fears might you be carrying about those phrases that are perhaps
still affecting your self-esteem?

"God's gonna get ya!"
"God will, or is, punishing me."
"The devil is after me!"
"I'm just a lowly sinner!"

These old notions can prey on our minds, can eat at our souls and remain so subtle that we hardly know they're there until we happen upon them in the safety of our awareness one day, or get hit suddenly in the face by our own low self-worth that thrives on such notions.

Cafeteria Style

So how do you know the right path? Look at life, with all of its choices. I believe it's a big cafeteria. Our needs for nourishment will change from day to day, year to year. The act of choosing is part of the way we learn. As we grow in self-esteem, we learn more about what feels right and what doesn't, what works and what feels "wrong."

We have many options, and that is good.

Trusting Our Inner Desires

A friend of mine once said she heard someone say, "Open up and let God out!" We often speak of letting someone or something in, as though we are incomplete. But suppose that within us is already the wholeness we need. We can start from our desires. Many of us have grown up with the consciousness that we were "sinners." We got the message that we were shameful and guilty of our desires. It was okay to dream, but not to fantasize. Dreams often had to do with visions. Fantasies often had to do with lust and greed or envy.

Whether or not you believe in the merit of your desires, there is a way to allow them to work for you so that you're not wasting energy fighting with them.

Sexual desires can be a way of tuning us in to energies that touch our experience beyond what is obvious. We can work through all sorts of barriers and learn much about respecting ourselves, building healthy boundaries and bonding with others.

Many times when people report having grown psychically or spiritually, they also experience a strong increase in sexual desire. I don't believe that this needs to be necessarily condemned or acted upon. It is energy. The sexual and the spiritual are one and the same, and one does not preclude the other. We can learn, we can expand in how we experience all of life.

In those times when we find ourselves wanting a lot of things, where someone would be tempted to call us "greedy," I say that those are self-esteem seeds. Those are indications that we have self-worth. We don't need to be shamed for wanting. We need to learn how to turn on, to work with energies so that what we want works "for goodness sake." The fact that we desire is a good sign.

And when we are sexually attracted, or we feel that someone is attracted toward us, those are positive signs, opportunities. If someone is attracted to us, then we can be sure we are putting out energy. We are being experienced by someone on levels that exceed our physical manifestation. If we are attracted to someone else, we are probably feeling something in a spiritual way as well as a physical way.

Now we may not be focused in a spiritual way. There may still be things to learn about handling this energy, learning that we are more than our bodies, that we are more than our concrete perceptions of the mundane. We are learning not to violate ourselves, learning what violation can be on more subtle levels. Moving into a more loving consciousness means growing beyond violence and violation. If we truly love ourselves, living with positive self-esteem, then there is no place for violence or violation in our philosophy or in our behavior.

It May Not Matter What You Call It!

I talk with agnostics and atheists, and I never assume that they are absent of beliefs. What I often imagine is that it is "the old," the dogma, the outdated expectations and explanations that are being rejected. Perhaps they are saying no to things that just do not make sense. Isn't that part of wholesome self-esteem? They refuse to lie to self, to others or to play games. "If they don't buy into the old beliefs, then what do they believe?" If you really want to know, then try asking sometime. You will get as many different answers as you find people to ask.

Okay. You've worked on getting comfortable with yourself, learning to more fully like and nurture yourself. You've learned more about how to grow in self-esteem as you grow in relationships with others. You've learned more about how you relate with places and things, and how your self-esteem is affected by how you interact with your environment. Now how do you put it all together?

The School Of Life

The introduction to *A Course In Miracles* states that . . . "This is a required course." In other words life is filled with many lessons and classrooms, and we are not exempt from learning. Fortunately, we have many choices about what we study, where and how we learn, but we all are here to learn.

Now, as you look at the fullness of your life, what do you perceive as the main lessons you've been here to learn? What are the classes you've taken? Who or what have been your teachers? Have there been lessons with themes?

Have there been lessons to repeat? Have there been teachers who were similar? How about those who have been different?

_____

_____

_____

_____

And what have been your texts, your sources of information, your places to explore whatever it is you know as "truth"? Are they books or tapes? Are they people?
    family
    friends
    therapist
    clergy
    a process of meditation
    Other:

_____

_____

Are the aspects of nature important dimensions of your "classroom"?

_____

_____

What have been the most comfortable "classrooms" as you go through the school of life?

_____

_____

What have been the most uncomfortable? Sometimes these are the class-rooms where we learn the most important lessons.

_____

_____

_____

What do you still need to learn in this school of life?

_____

_____

_____

Do you expect to be graded? _____ How would you grade yourself?

_____

_____

And what does "being tested" mean to you?
   "To see what I don't know."
   "To help me know what I know."
   "To help me see what I still need to learn."
   "To make me sweat."
   Other:

_____

_____

If you were to leave this life right now and find that someone was reviewing your life with you, what would you say to sum up the important aspects of your life? What would you say you've learned about self-esteem?

_____

_____

_____

Whether or not you believe in a sense of spirituality, perhaps it is still worth considering what you really believe about yourself.
   Work with some of the following questions:
   Are you worthy of abundance?

_____

_____

Are you doomed to live in poverty?

_____

_____

Are you in tune, intuitive? Do you have a right to know things beyond what is the obvious?

_____

What is the meaning or purpose of your life? Is there one?

_____

_____

What are you here to learn?

_____

_____

What are you here to do?

_____

_____

What is beyond this life for you?

_____

_____

How long will you be on this planet? Do you know? What do you believe?

_____

_____

Do you have a right to be loved?

_____

_____

What are your responsibilities?

_____

_____

Make It Yours

In the final analysis, it is your journey that counts. It is how you sort and solve the self-esteem puzzle, and what pieces you work with that lead you to the peace you seek and deserve. Make it yours.

Someone once told me he believed the purpose of therapy was "to get to the grief." I disagree! The purpose of therapy, of personal growth, recovery and so on, is to get to the joy.

So be about your life's work. Wear your uniform. Do your work, your teaching and learning, find what truth is yours to find, and use all of your experience to get to the joy!

ABOUT THE AUTHOR

Deborah Melaney Hazelton, a practicing mental health counselor, is president and founder of InnerSight Unlimited and author of *The Courage To See: Daily Affirmations For Healing The Shame Within*. InnerSight Unlimited is a consulting, counseling and educational organization offering services to the general public and the professional community.

Debbie has been involved extensively in her own personal growth and has worked professionally for seventeen years in the areas of self-improvement, human potential and development, recovery and human sexuality, including sexual abuse issues. She holds Bachelor's and Master's degrees in psychology and has completed advanced graduate training (Education Specialist Degree) in guidance and counseling.

Most recently, Debbie served as Contributing Editor for U.S. Journal periodicals, including *Changes* magazine, *FOCUS* magazine and *The U.S. Journal of Drug & Alcohol Dependence*. The former Outreach Coordinator for Health Communications, Inc. and U.S. Journal, Inc., she was also the editor of *CONTACT* newsletter, an information service of these two organizations. Debbie's professional career has included positions as college-level instructor, coordinator of student services for people living with disabilities and consultant to the program in human sexuality at the University of Miami Medical School, Department of Family Medicine.

In addition to her writing, Debbie is a sought-after speaker and can be heard nationally as a syndicated broadcast columnist. Her editorial features, entitled "The Courage To See," can be heard six times each day on AM radio stations around the country that are affiliated with WNN, a Pompano Beach, Florida-based radio station with a unique, 24-hour-a-day, self-help format.

If you would like additional information about InnerSight Unlimited and Debbie Hazelton's availability as a speaker, consultant or trainer for your community group or professional organization, please call or write directly to:

InnerSight Unlimited
265 South Federal Highway, Suite 125
Deerfield Beach, FL 33441
Phone: (305) 480-6014

New Books . . .
from Health Communications

ALTERNATIVE PATHWAYS TO HEALING: The Recovery Medicine Wheel
Kip Coggins, MSW
This book with its unique approach to recovery explains the concept of the medicine wheel — and how you can learn to live in harmony with yourself, with others and with the earth.

ISBN 1-55874-089-9   **$7.95**

UNDERSTANDING CO-DEPENDENCY
Sharon Wegscheider-Cruse, M.A., and Joseph R. Cruse, M.D.
The authors give us a basic understanding of co-dependency that everyone can use — what it is, how it happens, who is affected by it and what can be done for them.

ISBN 1-55874-077-5   **$7.95**

THE OTHER SIDE OF THE FAMILY:
A Book For Recovery From Abuse, Incest And Neglect
Ellen Ratner, Ed.M.
This workbook addresses the issues of the survivor — self-esteem, feelings, defenses, grieving, relationships and sexuality — and goes beyond to help them through the healing process.

ISBN 1-55874-110-0   **$13.95**

OVERCOMING PERFECTIONISM:
The Key To A Balanced Recovery
Ann W. Smith, M.S.
This book offers practical hints, together with a few lighthearted ones, as a guide toward learning to "live in the middle." It invites you to let go of your superhuman syndrome and find a balanced recovery.

ISBN 1-55874-111-9   **$8.95**

LEARNING TO SAY NO:
Establishing Healthy Boundaries
Carla Wills-Brandon, M.A.
If you grew up in a dysfunctional family, establishing boundaries is a difficult and risky decision. Where do you draw the line? Learn to recognize yourself as an individual who has the power to say no.

ISBN 1-55874-087-2   **$8.95**

3201 S.W. 15th Street,
Deerfield Beach, FL 33442-8190
1-800-851-9100

Health Communications, Inc.

Other Books By . . .
Health Communications

ADULT CHILDREN OF ALCOHOLICS
Janet Woititz

Over a year on *The New York Times* Best-Seller list, this book is the primer on Adult Children of Alcoholics.

ISBN 0-932194-15-X   **$6.95**

STRUGGLE FOR INTIMACY
Janet Woititz

Another best-seller, this book gives insightful advice on learning to love more fully.

ISBN 0-932194-25-7   **$6.95**

BRADSHAW ON: THE FAMILY: A Revolutionary Way of Self-Discovery
John Bradshaw

The host of the nationally televised series of the same name shows us how families can be healed and individuals can realize full potential.

ISBN 0-932194-54-0   **$9.95**

HEALING THE SHAME THAT BINDS YOU
John Bradshaw

This important book shows how toxic shame is the core problem in our compulsions and offers new techniques of recovery vital to all of us.

ISBN 0-932194-86-9   **$9.95**

HEALING THE CHILD WITHIN: Discovery and Recovery for
Adult Children of Dysfunctional Families — Charles Whitfield, M.D.

Dr. Whitfield defines, describes and discovers how we can reach our Child Within to heal and nurture our woundedness.

ISBN 0-932194-40-0   **$8.95**

A GIFT TO MYSELF: A Personal Guide To Healing My Child Within
Charles L. Whitfield, M.D.

Dr. Whitfield provides practical guidelines and methods to work through the pain and confusion of being an Adult Child of a dysfunctional family.

ISBN 1-55874-042-2   **$11.95**

HEALING TOGETHER: A Guide To Intimacy And Recovery For
Co-dependent Couples — Wayne Kritsberg, M.A.

This is a practical book that tells the reader why he or she gets into dysfunctional and painful relationships, and then gives a concrete course of action on how to move the relationship toward health.

ISBN 1-55784-053-8   **$8.95**

3201 S.W. 15th Street,
Deerfield Beach, FL 33442-8190
1-800-851-9100

Health Communications, Inc.

Daily Affirmation Books from . . . Health Communications

GENTLE REMINDERS FOR CO-DEPENDENTS: Daily Affirmations
Mitzi Chandler

With insight and humor, Mitzi Chandler takes the co-dependent and the adult child through the year. Gentle Reminders is for those in recovery who seek to enjoy the miracle each day brings.

ISBN 1-55874-020-1   **$6.95**

TIME FOR JOY: Daily Affirmations
Ruth Fishel

With quotations, thoughts and healing energizing affirmations these daily messages address the fears and imperfections of being human, guiding us through self-acceptance to a tangible peace and the place within where there is *time for joy*.

ISBN 0-932194-82-6   **$6.95**

AFFIRMATIONS FOR THE INNER CHILD
Rokelle Lerner

This book contains powerful messages and helpful suggestions aimed at adults who have unfinished childhood issues. By reading it daily we can end the cycle of suffering and move from pain into recovery.

ISBN 1-55874-045-6   **$6.95**

DAILY AFFIRMATIONS: For Adult Children of Alcoholics
Rokelle Lerner

Affirmations are a way to discover personal awareness, growth and spiritual potential, and self-regard. Reading this book gives us an opportunity to nurture ourselves, learn who we are and what we want to become.

ISBN 0-932194-47-3
(Little Red Book)   **$6.95**
(New Cover Edition)   **$6.95**

SOOTHING MOMENTS: Daily Meditations For Fast-Track Living
Bryan E. Robinson, Ph.D.

This is designed for those leading fast-paced and high-pressured lives who need time out each day to bring self-renewal, joy and serenity into their lives.

ISBN 1-55874-075-9   **$6.95**

3201 S.W. 15th Street,
Deerfield Beach, FL 33442-8190
1-800-851-9100

Health Communications, Inc.

YOU CAN SUCCEED!

With Changes Magazine — America's Leading Recovery Publication

Receive A Free Issue Now!

Discover the magazine that's giving thousands of people across the United States the vital self-healing tools they need to reach their personal recovery potential.

Each copy of Changes brings you new information on today's recovery issues like self-esteem, sexuality, co-dependency, relationships, and the inner child. Plus you'll receive news on support groups, innovative recovery techniques, and insights from featured personalities like Oprah Winfrey, John Bradshaw, and Leo Buscaglia.

TAKE THIS SPECIAL OPPORTUNITY TO RECEIVE A FREE ISSUE OF CHANGES
BY RETURNING THE COUPON BELOW.

Yes, please send me my free issue of **Changes** Magazine — a $3.75 newsstand value! If I decide to subscribe, I'll pay your invoice for $18.00 for a one-year subscription (6 issues including my complimentary issue) and save 20% off the newsstand price. If I don't choose to subscribe, I'll simply write "Cancel" on the invoice, return it to you, and owe nothing.

Name _____
(please print)

Address _____ Apt. _____

City _____ State _____ Zip_____
FCCHG1

☐ Please add my name to your mailing list for advance notice of conferences in my area plus catalogs of recovery books, audio tapes, and special gifts.

SEND TO: The U.S. Journal Inc.
Subscriptions
3201 SW 15th St.
Deerfield Beach, FL 33442-8190